maison ikkoku 4

STORY AND ART BY RUMIKO TAKAHASHI

TABLE OF CONTENTS

PART ONE
CATCH OF THE DAY

OKAY NOW... YOU HOLD THE RACKET SO THE FACE IS LIKE SO...

IGNORE YOU?! BUT... BUT I WOULD NEVER...

AFTER YOU COMPLETELY IGNORED ME FOR A WHOLE YEAR, IT'S PRETTY STRANGE THAT YOU SUDDENLY DECIDE TO START COACHING ME.

THE... THE CHASE?

LOOK, WHY DON'T YOU JUST DROP THE CHARADE AND CUT TO THE CHASE.

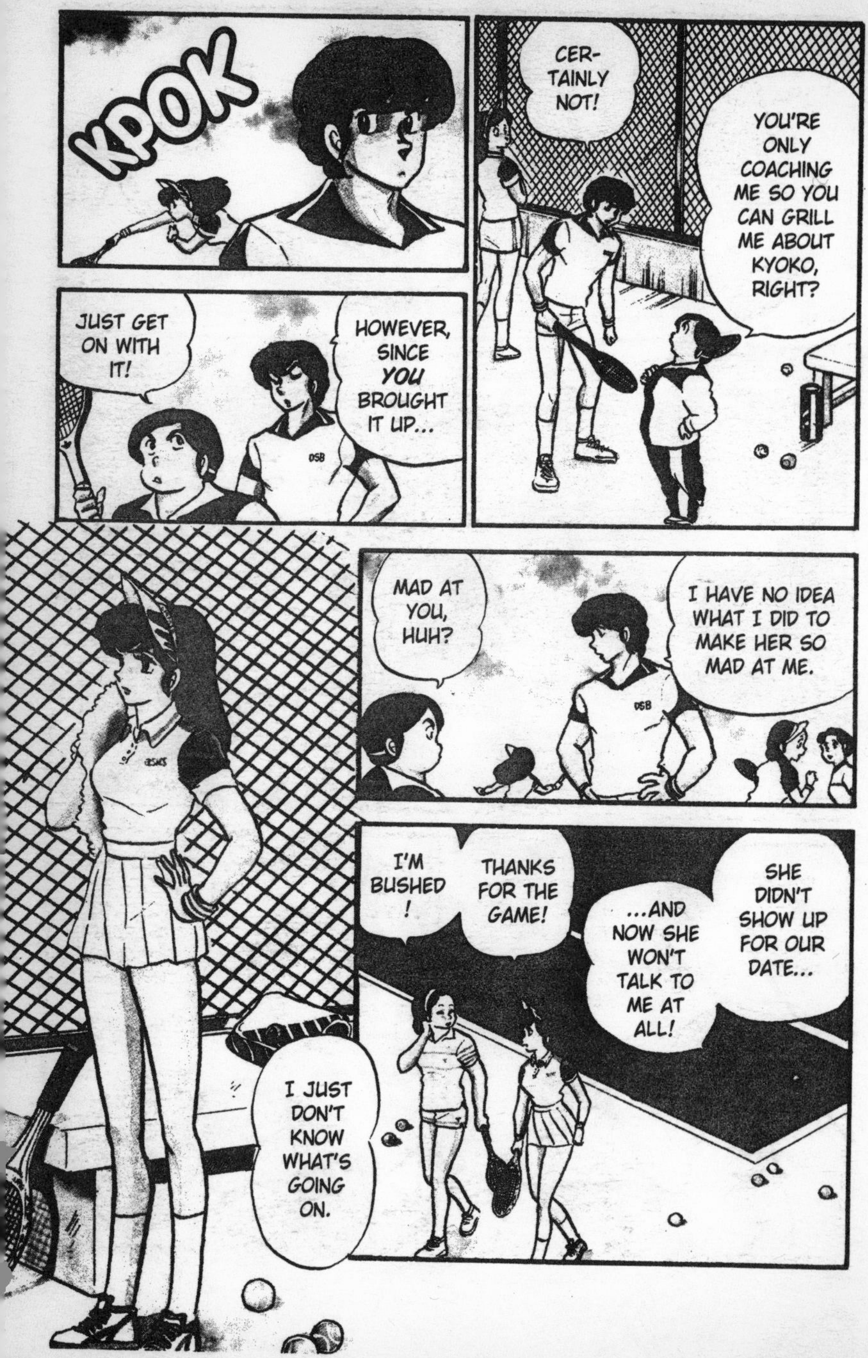
KPOK
YOU'RE ONLY COACHING ME SO YOU CAN GRILL ME ABOUT KYOKO, RIGHT?
CER-TAINLY NOT!
HOWEVER, SINCE YOU BROUGHT IT UP...
JUST GET ON WITH IT!
I HAVE NO IDEA WHAT I DID TO MAKE HER SO MAD AT ME.
MAD AT YOU, HUH?
SHE DIDN'T SHOW UP FOR OUR DATE...
...AND NOW SHE WON'T TALK TO ME AT ALL!
THANKS FOR THE GAME!
I'M BUSHED!
I JUST DON'T KNOW WHAT'S GOING ON.

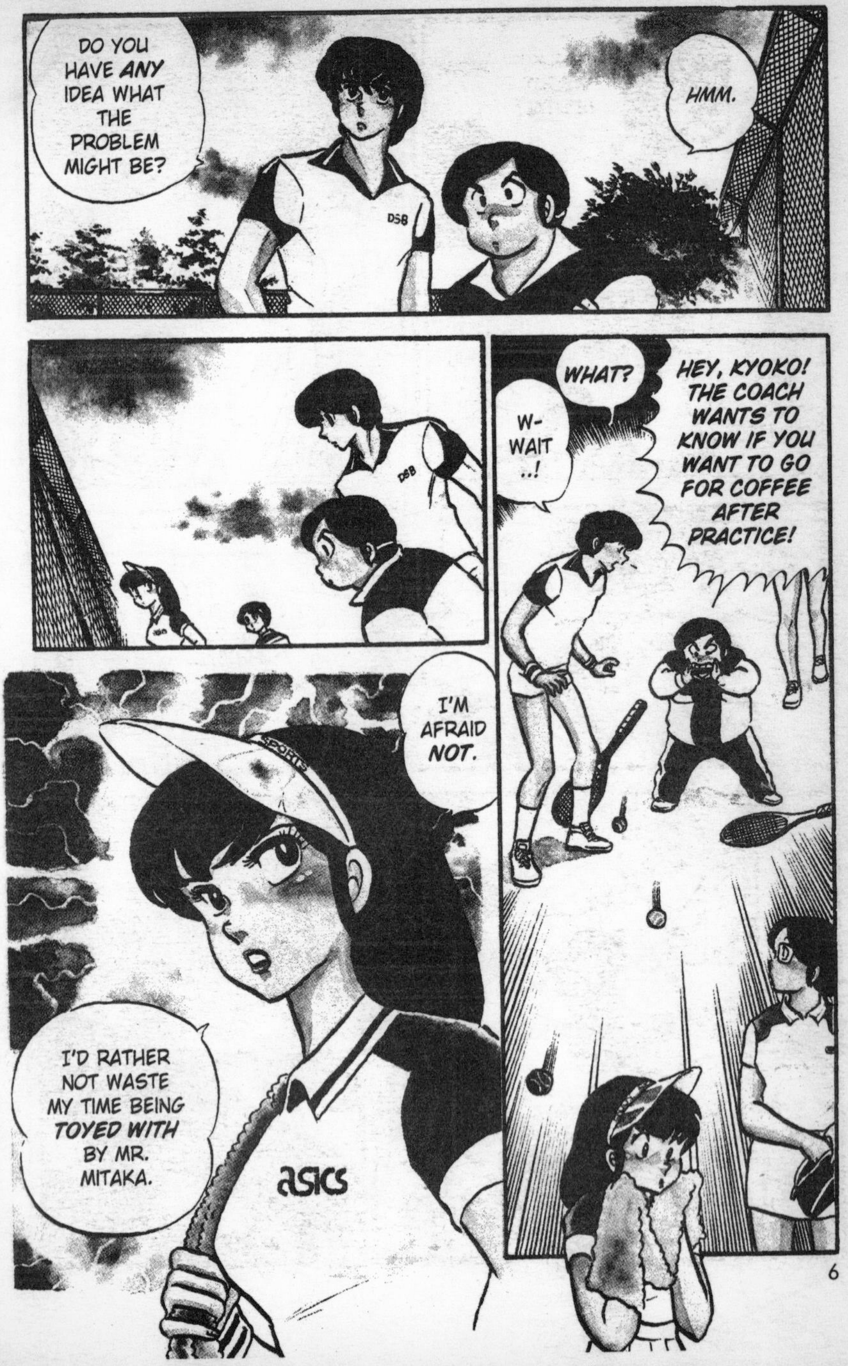
DO YOU HAVE *ANY* IDEA WHAT THE PROBLEM MIGHT BE?
HMM.
I'M AFRAID *NOT*.
I'D RATHER NOT WASTE MY TIME BEING *TOYED WITH* BY MR. MITAKA.
asics
HEY, KYOKO! THE COACH WANTS TO KNOW IF YOU WANT TO GO FOR COFFEE AFTER PRACTICE!
WHAT?
W-WAIT ..!

THAT WAS TOTALLY UNNECESSARY!

TALK ABOUT BRUTAL!

WOW.

HMPH!

...

...

I'M TALKING ABOUT *YOU*, MRS. ICHINOSE!

IT SURE WAS — DID YOU *HEAR* HER?

OH, YEAH?

GODAI IS, TOO.

YOU'RE NOT THE ONLY ONE GETTING THE DEEP FREEZE.

OH, QUIT YOUR WHINING.

MORE AND MORE...

...I'M HAVING A HARD TIME UNDERSTANDING KYOKO.

BUT JEEZ, SHE SEES MITAKA ALL THE TIME!

...I GUESS SHE DOESN'T LIKE ME SEEING KOZUE.

THAT'S KIND OF SELF-CENTERED, ISN'T IT?

I CAN'T THINK OF ANY OTHER REASON FOR IT, SO...

HECK, SHE HASN'T EVEN *TALKED* TO ME FOR A WHILE.

...BUT SHE *STILL* GETS ALL BENT OUTTA SHAPE OVER ME HANGING OUT WITH KOZUE.

NOT VERY DAMN FAIR!

BESIDES, IT'S NOT LIKE I'VE REALLY GOTTEN ANYWHERE WITH HER...

NOW I'M STARTING TO GET *MAD*.

UH-OH...

I'M NOT A TOY FOR YOU TO PLAY WITH, KYOKO!!

DAMN IT!

...NOBODY WAS LISTENING.

I... I SURE HOPE...

...

...THIS IS JUST GOING TO GET WORSE IF I SIT HERE BROODING.

WELL...

EH?

OH, GOOD — I THOUGHT EVERYONE MIGHT BE OUT.

MAY AS WELL SHOW UP FOR AFTERNOON CLASSES.

WHAT THE HECK...

TUMP

AW, IT'S NOT A VERY IMPORTANT CLASS.

THANK YOU, BUT WEREN'T YOU ON YOUR WAY TO CLASS?

DO YOU KNOW WHERE SHE MIGHT BE?

Y-YOU'RE KYOKO'S MOTHER!!

SNAP

M-MY NAME IS YUSAKU GODAI, MA'AM.

SAY, YOUNG MAN...

I SHOULD BE NICE TO HER. IT'LL PAY OFF EVENTUALLY...

HM?

WOULD YOU HAPPEN TO KNOW IF MY DAUGHTER HAS ANYONE SHE'S INTERESTED IN?

THAT'S... UH... KINDA HARD TO SAY...

WELL, UH...

WELL, FOR INSTANCE, HAVE YOU SEEN HER GOING OUT WITH ANYONE?

I MEAN, YOU MUST KNOW SOMETHING SINCE YOU LIVE AT MAISON IKKOKU.

THAT'S ALL FOR TODAY, CLASS.

I'M A MAN!

IF THERE WERE AT LEAST *SOME* MEN IN HER LIFE, I MIGHT BE ABLE TO RELAX.

10

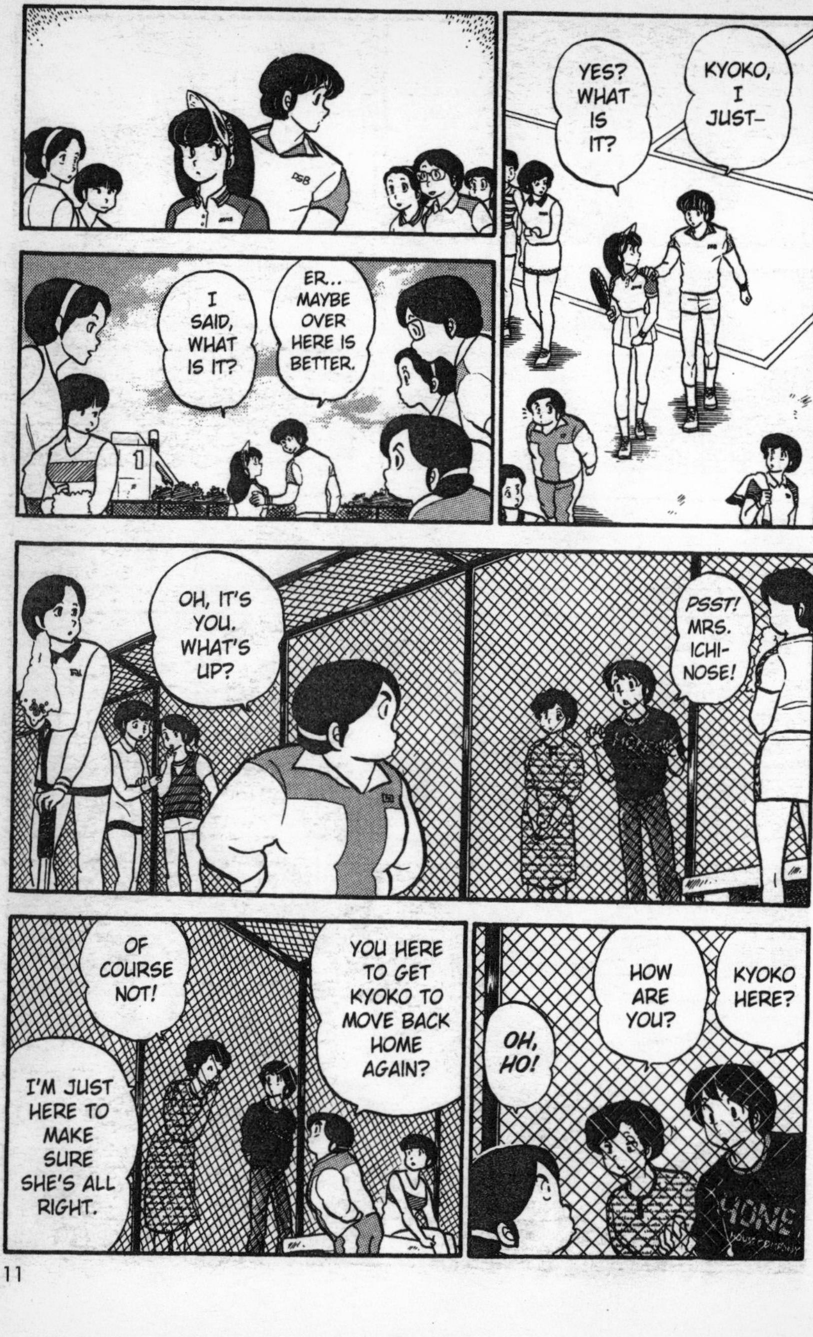
KYOKO, I JUST-
YES? WHAT IS IT?
I SAID, WHAT IS IT?
ER.. MAYBE OVER HERE IS BETTER.
PSST! MRS. ICHI-NOSE!
OH, IT'S YOU. WHAT'S UP?
KYOKO HERE?
HOW ARE YOU?
OH, HO!
YOU HERE TO GET KYOKO TO MOVE BACK HOME AGAIN?
OF COURSE NOT!
I'M JUST HERE TO MAKE SURE SHE'S ALL RIGHT.

THEY SAY THE HOTTER THE FIGHTING, THE HOTTER THE LOVE.

DOES IT LOOK LIKE THEY'RE ARGUING?

HE'S THE COACH OF OUR TENNIS CLUB.

WHO... IS... *THAT?*

OH, YEAH. THEY GO OUT ALL THE TIME.

HE'S EVEN PROPOSED TO HER!

EXCUSE ME... IS... MY DAUGHTER SEEING THAT YOUNG MAN?

12

SO KYOKO *DOES* HAVE A MAN IN HER LIFE!

OH, *MY!*

WHAT DO YOU KNOW ABOUT THIS MAN?

WHY DON'T YOU ASK *YOURSELF* THAT QUESTION?

PLEASE. I ONLY WANT TO KNOW WHY YOU'RE SO ANGRY WITH ME.

WHAT'S HIS FAMILY LIKE?

HOW OLD IS HE?

OH? THEN ASK THAT *FRIEND* OF YOURS!

I HAVE! BUT I HAVE NO IDEA...

WHAT?

THE ONE YOU WERE BEING SO *COZY* WITH IN THE DOG GROOMING SALON.

OH!

OH, **WELL** THEN. I SUPPOSE IT'S FINE FOR YOU TO PAW WOMEN YOU DON'T EVEN **KNOW**.

BUT KYOKO, I DON'T EVEN **KNOW** HER!

I DID INDEED.

YOU... SAW THAT?

THAT'S QUITE ALL RIGHT. YOU DON'T NEED TO MAKE UP AN EXCUSE.

IT... ER...

WELL... UH...

CAN YOU NOW?

NO, I... LOOK, I CAN EXPLAIN EVERY- THING...

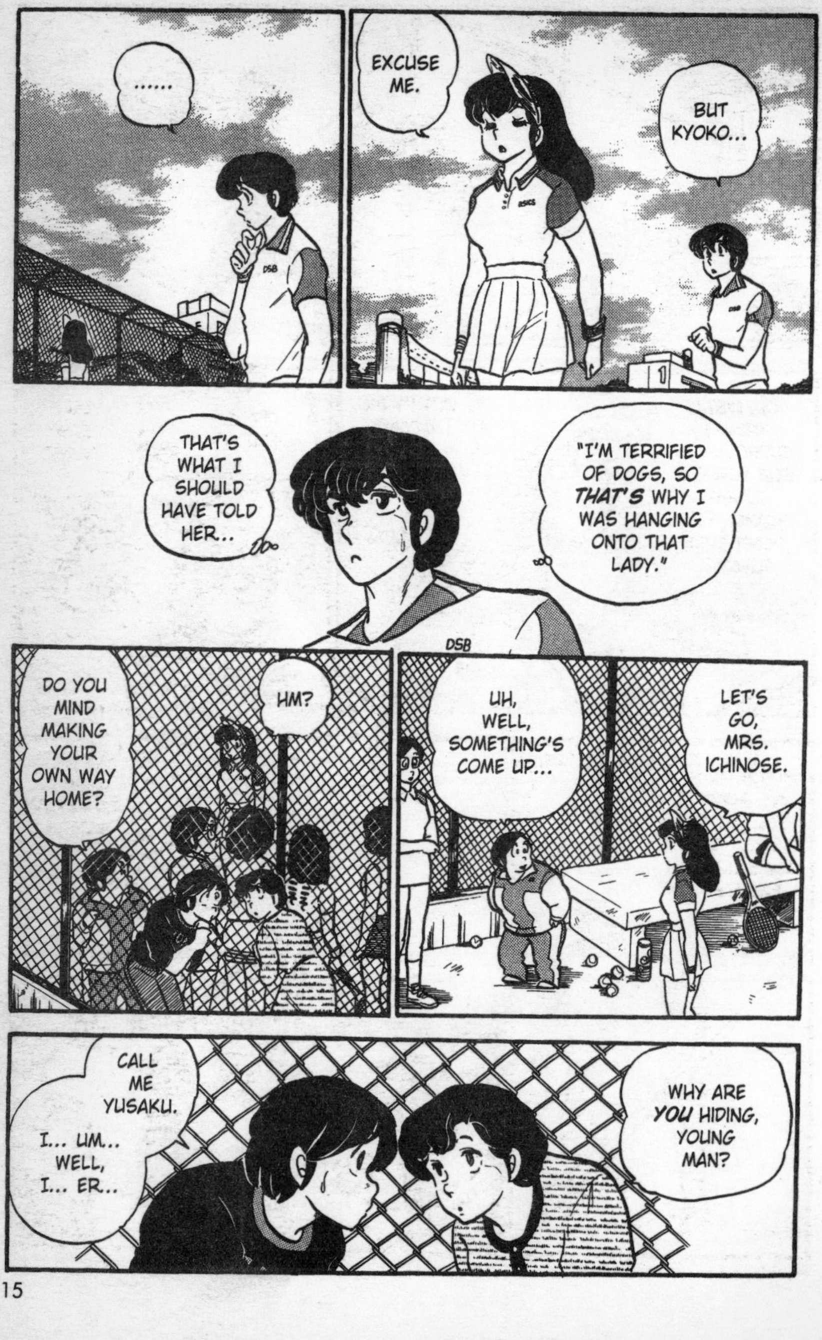
......
EXCUSE ME.
BUT KYOKO...
THAT'S WHAT I SHOULD HAVE TOLD HER...
"I'M TERRIFIED OF DOGS, SO *THAT'S* WHY I WAS HANGING ONTO THAT LADY."
DO YOU MIND MAKING YOUR OWN WAY HOME?
HM?
UH, WELL, SOMETHING'S COME UP...
LET'S GO, MRS. ICHINOSE.
CALL ME YUSAKU.
I... UM... WELL, I... ER...
WHY ARE *YOU* HIDING, YOUNG MAN?

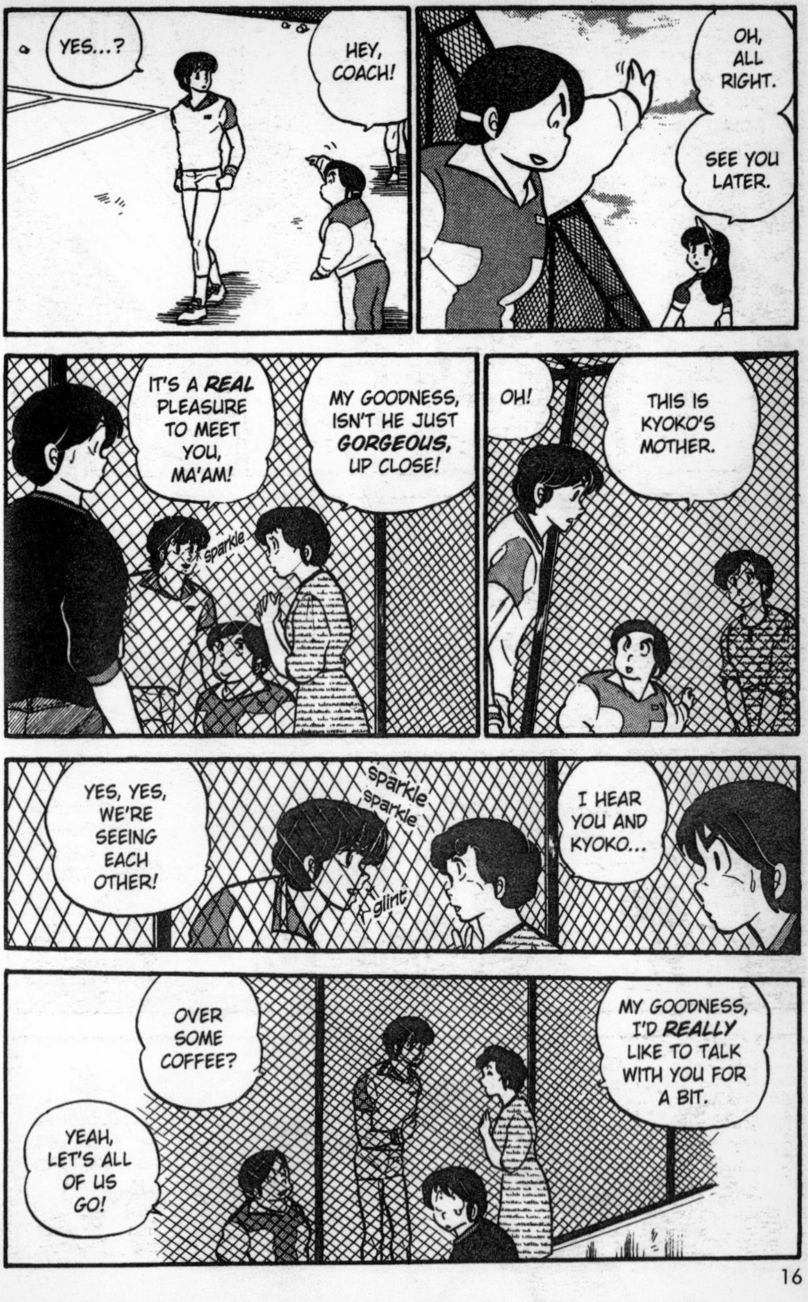
OH, ALL RIGHT.
SEE YOU LATER.
HEY, COACH!
YES...?
THIS IS KYOKO'S MOTHER.
OH!
MY GOODNESS, ISN'T HE JUST GORGEOUS, UP CLOSE!
IT'S A REAL PLEASURE TO MEET YOU, MA'AM!
sparkle
I HEAR YOU AND KYOKO...
YES, YES, WE'RE SEEING EACH OTHER!
sparkle sparkle
glint
MY GOODNESS, I'D REALLY LIKE TO TALK WITH YOU FOR A BIT.
OVER SOME COFFEE?
YEAH, LET'S ALL OF US GO!

I'M READY TO MAKE A REAL COMMITMENT, IF ONLY KYOKO WOULD GIVE ME THE OKAY...

REALLY? FOR A WHOLE YEAR ALREADY?

WHY AM I EVEN HERE?

WHAT ARE YOU ALL GRUMPY ABOUT?

...... NO, NO! WELL, MAYBE... AT TIMES....

BUT DON'T YOU FIND MY DAUGHTER DIFFICULT TO DEAL WITH SOMETIMES?

WHY WOULD YOU—

IT IS *NOT!*

ANOTHER WOMAN, I BET!

WELL, IT'S... UH...

SO WHAT WERE YOU TWO FIGHTING ABOUT TODAY?

...YOU SHOULDN'T JUDGE A BOOK BY ITS COVER.

YOU KNOW...

AW, C'MON... YOU SURE LOOK LIKE THE TYPE.

OH, ABSO-LUTELY!

YOU BELIEVE ME, DON'T YOU, MA'AM?

HEAVENS, NO! IT DOESN'T MATTER ANYMORE!

SO THERE'S NO PROBLEM WITH HER STAYING ON AS THE MANAGER?

HAD I KNOWN ABOUT THIS SOONER, I WOULDN'T HAVE HAD TO TRY AND FORCE KYOKO TO QUIT HER JOB.

OH, I'M *SO* RELIEVED!

SURE — THIS IS JUST *GREAT* NEWS.

GREAT NEWS, EH, GODAI?

NOW WHAT DO YOU WANT?!

MOM ...?

RRIINNGG

DO AS YOU WISH.

...I WON'T BE TRYING TO GET YOU TO QUIT YOUR JOB ANYMORE.

?

NOW, DEAR, DON'T BE SO DEFENSIVE.

NOTHING, DEAR. NOTHING.

WHAT ARE YOU UP TO, MOTHER?!

I KNOW WE'VE HAD OUR DIFFERENCES LATELY, BUT...

AFTER ALL, YOU'RE AN ADULT NOW — IT REALLY ISN'T OUR PLACE TO TELL YOU WHAT TO DO.

LIKE WHAT?

I DON'T LIKE IT.

WHAT IN THE WORLD ...?

YOU HAVEN'T EVEN *MET* HIM YET!

THAT COACH WHAT'S-HIS-NAME.

Ching

SOUNDS LIKE SOUR GRAPES TO ME.

HE'S PROBABLY RUNNING AROUND WITH A DOZEN WOMEN.

THAT'S THE PART I DON'T LIKE.

AND HE'S A *HUNK.*

THERE'S NO ROOM FOR COMPLAINT—

—ECONOMICALLY, EDUCATIONALLY, OR PERSONALITY-WISE.

THEN WHAT KIND OF MAN *WOULD* YOU AGREE WITH?!

I'VE JUST GOT KYOKO'S BEST INTERESTS IN MIND, THAT'S ALL!

IF YOU REMEMBER, *YOU* HAD A LOT TO SAY BACK THEN TOO!

EVEN WHEN SHE MARRIED THAT WONDERFUL SOICHIRO, YOU COMPLAINED ABOUT HIS AGE AND ANYTHING ELSE YOU COULD THINK OF!!

......

WELL, I'M SURE KYOKO IS ALL FOR IT!

YOU'RE NOT THE ONE GETTING MARRIED.

HE'S THE CATCH OF THE DAY, IF YOU ASK ME.

WELL, I HIGHLY APPROVE THIS TIME!

20

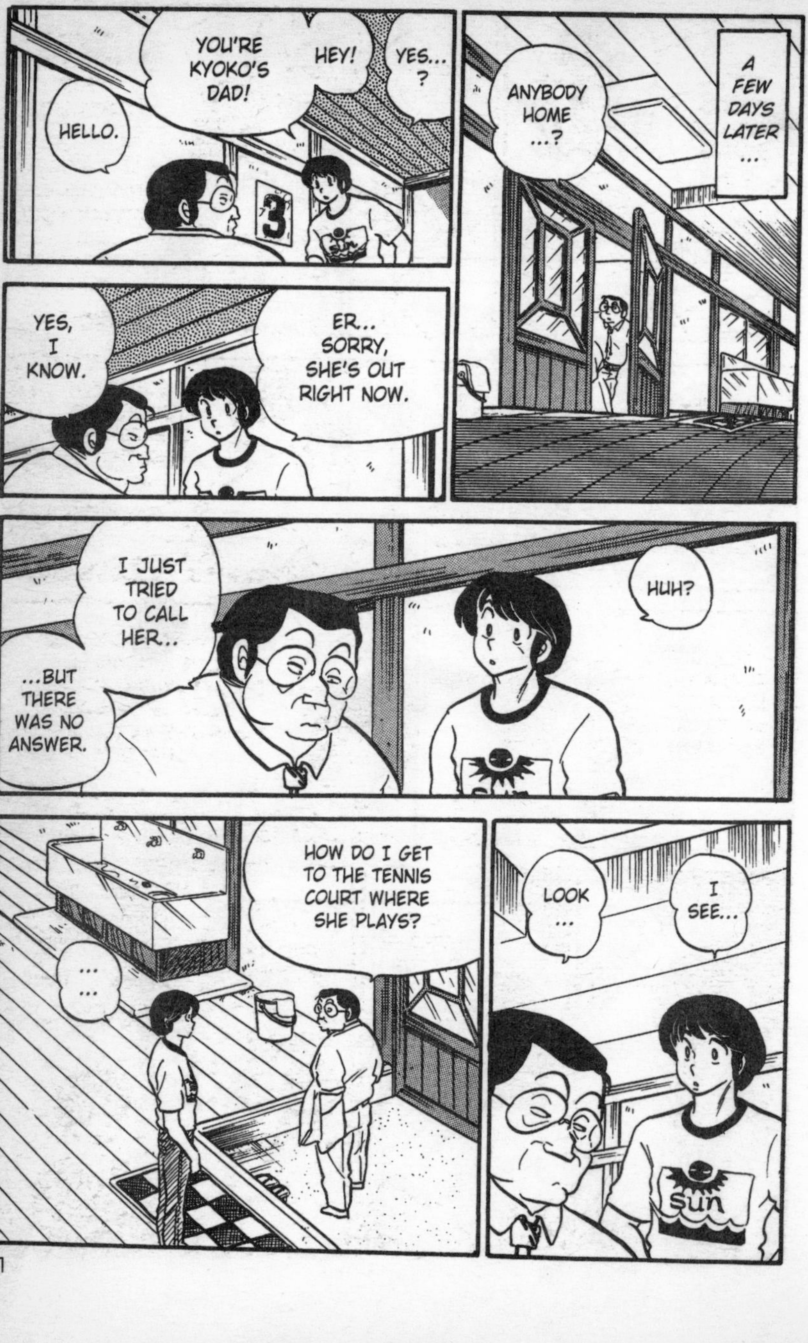
A FEW DAYS LATER ...
ANYBODY HOME ...?
YES... ?
HEY!
YOU'RE KYOKO'S DAD!
HELLO.
ER... SORRY, SHE'S OUT RIGHT NOW.
YES, I KNOW.
HUH?
I JUST TRIED TO CALL HER...
...BUT THERE WAS NO ANSWER.
I SEE...
LOOK ...
HOW DO I GET TO THE TENNIS COURT WHERE SHE PLAYS?
... ...

......

......

THANKS FOR TAKING ME ALL THE WAY HERE.

NO PROBLEM... I WASN'T DOING ANYTHING, ANYWAY.

PRACTICE ...?

WHAT TIME DOES PRACTICE START?

ER...

OH, WELL...

IS THAT A FACT...

THEY DON'T PRACTICE ON SATURDAYS.

...

SUN

MITAKA?

YOU KNOW SOME GUY NAMED MITAKA?

WELL, YEAH... SORT OF.

YES?

CALL ME YUSAKU.

SAY, KID...

22

WELL...

IT'S KINDA HARD TO SAY...

SO... WHAT DOES KYOKO THINK ABOUT ALL THIS?

REALLY?

I JUST DON'T LIKE THE FACT THAT HE'S SUPPOSED TO BE A REAL LADY-KILLER...

BUT I'M *NOT* AN "OUTSIDER"!

LOOKING AT IT FROM AN OUTSIDER'S POINT OF VIEW, YOU THINK THIS MITAKA GUY CAN MAKE MY KYOKO HAPPY?

THOSE "GQ" TYPES IN GENERAL ARE, WELL...

I THINK I CAN UNDERSTAND HOW YOU FEEL.

YOU THINK SO, TOO?

OH, YEAH... I AGREE...

I MEAN, IF HE'S GOT A LOT OF LADY FRIENDS, IT MIGHT BE HARD ON KYOKO.

YOU CAN CALL ME YUSAKU, MR. CHIGUSA!

YOU REALLY THINK SO, KID? LOOKING AT IT FROM THE POINT OF VIEW OF A DISPASSIONATE THIRD PARTY?

BESIDES, I COULDN'T JUST LEAVE YOU ALONE WHEN YOU'RE FEELING SO BAD, HUH?

NO, NO!

MUSTN'T BE ANY FUN, DRINKING WITH AN OLD COOT LIKE ME...

SORRY, KID.

SURE YOU DON'T HAVE SOMETHING BETTER TO DO?

MALE BONDING BY EXCESSIVE DRINKING — THAT'S THE WAY!

HER MOM'S A LOST CAUSE— BETTER GO FOR DAD!

I GUESS SO...

DAUGHTERS ARE SO PRECIOUS.

CALL ME YUSAKU.

AND OF *COURSE* I DON'T HAVE ANY CHILDREN.

HEY, KID... YOU GOT ANY CHILDREN?

HA, HA, HEH.

AHA HA HA! YOU THINK SO, HUH?! AHA HA HA!

IT'S NOT LOOKS THAT MATTER, IT'S *PERSONALITY*...

YEAH... NO KIDDING.

IT REALLY MAKES YOU THINK "IF IT COMES DOWN TO THAT, I'M NOT GONNA LET HER GET SWEPT AWAY BY SOME... SOME PRETTY BOY!"

24

HUH?

THE ANSWER IS **NO**!

YOU'RE SO NAÏVE.

DAMN RIGHT!

I'M NOT LETTING **ANYONE** HAVE MY KYOKO AGAIN!

GLUG GLUG

THUD

GULP

OH, DADDY...

WHAT **ARE** YOU DOING HERE?

AND WHY ARE YOU OUT DRINKING WITH YUSAKU?

MY FATHER?

WHAT?

HE SAYS HE'S NOT GOING TO MOVE UNTIL YOU SHOW UP.

YEAH...

RRIINNGG

OH... YUSAKU?

HELLO?

SAY... HAVE YOU BEEN DRINKING?

C'MON, IT'S ALL RIGHT.

COME ON, FATHER ... UP YOU GO.

KYOKO!

YUSAKU ...?

GODDA GO'N GET KYO- -HIC- -KO...!

I'M RIGHT HERE.

I DON' WAN'YA GETTIN' MARRIED 'GAIN!

YOU LISHENING, KYOKO?!

WHAT *ARE* YOU TALKING ABOUT?!

I NEVER SAID ANYTHING ABOUT GETTING REMARRIED!!

DARN OL' COOT!

HEY!! WADD'R YOU TWO DOIN' UP THERE, HUH?

26

PART TWO
TURN THE OTHER CHEEK

IS THERE SOMETHING YOU WANTED TO TALK ABOUT?

SO WHAT ABOUT KYOKO *NOW*?

I... I DON'T KNOW HOW TO SAY IT...

IT BUGS ME WHEN YOU JUST SIT THERE LIKE THAT.

...
...

...
...

YOU REALLY THINK SHE'S JEALOUS?

COULD A WOMAN GET JEALOUS ABOUT A GUY SHE DOESN'T CARE ABOUT?

WHAT *ELSE* DO YOU EVER TALK ABOUT?

AKEMI, HOW'D YOU KNOW?

28

YOU'VE BEEN EATING AT KOZUE'S, LIKE, TWICE A WEEK.

I MEAN, LOOK...

...

...

MAYBE SHE JUST DOESN'T LIKE *YOU*, YOU WORM.

WELL, SHE MAKES ALL THESE COMMENTS WHEN I SEE KOZUE.

BUT YOU KEEP SAYING, "THERE'S NOTHING BETWEEN US!"

STAB STAB

EXPLOITER.

COWARD.

WISHY-WASHY

GUT-LESS.

USER.

G' NIGHT!

WORM.

VOOOM

"MAYBE SHE JUST DOESN'T LIKE YOU..."

THAT'S NICE.

WELL, I'M OFF!

IT'S TIME I FINALLY MADE MY DECISION.

OH! YES?

HEY, KYOKO!

...
...

BUT I LOVE SWEEPING... REALLY!

DIDN'T YOU JUST SWEEP THIS MORNING?

UM... SWEEPING?

WHAT ARE YOU DOING OUT HERE?

WHY, THANK YOU.

THOUGHT I'D BRING THE RENT EARLY.

MAYBE SHE DOESN'T COMPLETELY HATE ME.

FUNNY HOW SHE'S ALWAYS SWEEPING THE FRONT WHEN I HAVE A DATE.

I'VE GOT TO LET KOZUE KNOW WITHOUT HURTING HER.

GENTLY...

I'VE GOT TO DO SOMETHING!

hee
hee
hee
hee

I HAVE TO TELL HER NOW!

HM? OH... REALLY?

WHAT'S WRONG, YUSAKU? YOU DON'T LOOK HAPPY.

...UM...

WELL... YOU SEE...

YES?

KOZUE, I DON'T KNOW HOW TO SAY THIS, BUT...

I HAVE TO BREAK UP WITH YOU.

BUT... WHY?

WH-WHAT?

......

I'VE BEEN THINKING ABOUT IT FOR A WHILE NOW. BUT I COULDN'T BRING MYSELF TO HURT YOU.

PLEASE! BE QUIET!

I'VE TRIED TO BE EVERYTHING FOR YOU! BUT, NOW YOU—

BUT... BUT HOW CAN YOU DO THIS? WHY?

ANSWER ME!

I'VE EVEN TOLD MY PARENTS ABOUT YOU! WHAT'S HAPPENED?!

ANYWAY, THIS BAND'S ACT IS, LIKE, SO GROSS!

...I'VE... GOTTEN ENGAGED!

THE TRUTH IS, I'VE...

DO THEY REALLY BRING A PIG'S HEAD ON STAGE?

ZIP

ZIP

YOU WERE **TWO-TIMING** ME?!

YOU... **WHAT**?!

HWOOOOOO

I WON'T MAKE IT THAT **EASY**!!

I WON'T LET YOU GO!

YOU **WORM**!

HOW COULD YOU BE SO... CRUEL?

Y-YEAH, ME N-NEITHER.

JEEZ. I NEVER THOUGHT I'D SEE ANYTHING LIKE THAT.

BWAMM!

...

33

I... UH... I GUESS NOT.

COULDN'T SHE TELL HE WAS JUST USING HER?

YEAH...

JUST... HORRIBLE.

WHAT A HORRIBLE MAN!

I MEAN... WHO COULD?

YEAH. I COULDN'T HANDLE THAT.

...

THAT'S IT FOR TODAY'S PRACTICE.

...

WELL ...

NOT YET, I'M AFRAID.

HAVE YOU MADE UP WITH KYOKO?

YES?

HEY, COACH.

PRETTY CONFIDENT, AREN'T YOU?

I'M GOING TO GIVE KYOKO SOME TIME TO CALM DOWN.

IT'S NOT THAT I'M CONTENT, REALLY.

SO WHY DO YOU LOOK SO CONTENT?

I'VE JUST DECIDED NOT TO HURRY.

DAMN CONFIDENT.

DOESN'T THE FACT THAT SHE'S JEALOUS OF ME SAY SOMETHING?

9

hmph!

asics

glint

COULD YOU STOP PEEKING OVER?

HE WON'T WANT YOU FOREVER!

YOU'VE SURE GOT NERVE.

heh heh heh

WELL, I'LL SEE YOU LATER.

I DON'T NEED A MAN IN MY LIFE ANYMORE.

I'LL BE FINE.

OH?

...

...

YOU'RE SO STUBBORN! HOW LONG DO YOU PLAN TO BE MAD?

NOW THAT HURTS!

I'M NOT THAT KIND OF WOMAN!

THAT'S VULGAR?

DOESN'T YOUR *BODY* EVER CRY OUT FOR A MAN?

DON'T BE SO VULGAR!

NO, NO, IT WON'T GO LIKE THAT. I'M SURE OF IT.

HOW COULD YOU LIE TO ME?!

-SIGH-

...WHY SHOULD IT BE SO COMPLICATED?

EVEN IF I DO BREAK UP WITH HER..

I NEVER EVEN KISSED HER!

YOU'RE NOT EATING WITH THE NANAO FAMILY TONIGHT?

HI... I'M HOME.

DINNER-TIME, MR. SOICHIRO.

...

I'VE GOT TO STOP EATING OVER THERE.

SHE'S RIGHT.

CAN YOU BELIEVE HIM, MR. SOICHIRO?

DIDN'T EVEN ANSWER!

WELL!

K.L.K.

nnnn?

...
...

nnnn?

WHY DOESN'T HE JUST PICK A REGULAR NIGHT OF THE WEEK TO GO OVER THERE?

...
...

piro

IS IT KOZUE?

PROB- ABLY ANOTHER DINNER INVITATION.

YUSAKU! TELEPHONE!

THE NEXT DAY...

38

UH-HUH.

HI.

hsst

THANKS, BUT I'LL HAVE TO BEG OFF TONIGHT.

WHY DO I BOTHER EVEN THINKING ABOUT THAT HOPELESS...

YEAH.

SURE.

SEE...

I FEEL LIKE I'VE BEEN MOOCHING OFF YOU.

TOMORROW?

SORRY, BUT I DON'T THINK SO.

...
...

I JUST NEED TO STRAIGHTEN OUT MY PRIORITIES, YOU KNOW?

NO, THERE'S NO HEAVY MEANING HERE.

YES?

HEY, KYOKO?

NO, IT CAN'T BE.

IS IT BECAUSE OF MY SARCASTIC REMARKS?

KLIK

I WONDER WHAT'S HAPPENED?

YOU COULD AT LEAST PRETEND!

WELL, I COULDN'T HELP OVERHEARING, THE ROOM BEING WHERE IT IS AND ALL.

WERE YOU EAVES-DROPPING AGAIN?

WHAT'S UP WITH YUSAKU AND THIS "PRIORITIES" STUFF?

I HAVEN'T SAID *THAT* MUCH!

MAYBE YOU WORE HIM DOWN BY PICKING ON HIM SO OFTEN!

I COULDN'T HELP OVER-HEARING.

AND HOW DO YOU KNOW HE SAID THAT?

IT'S NOT MY FAULT! HE'S THE ONE WHO SAID HE HAD TO STRAIGHTEN OUT HIS PRIORITIES!

YOU'RE THE TYPE WHO CAN CRUSH A MAN WITH ONE BAD MOOD.

40

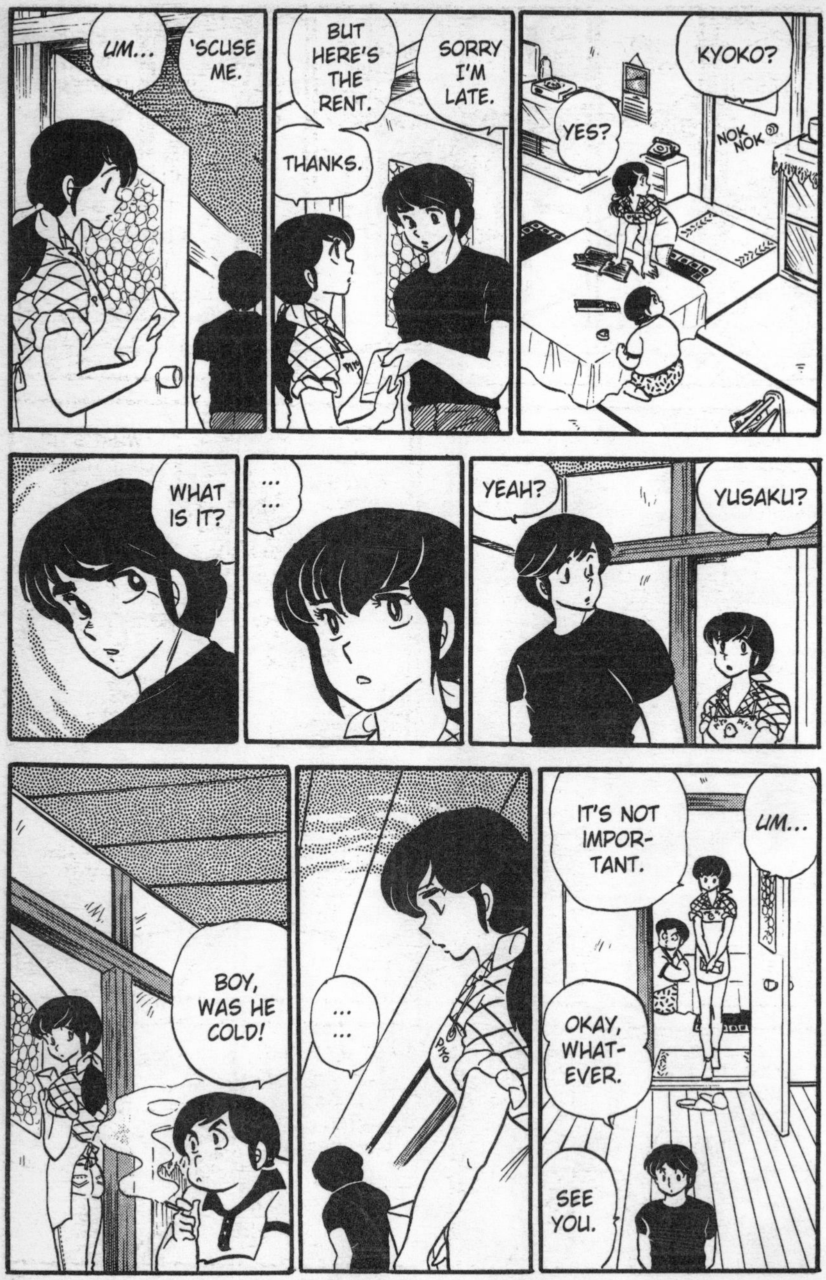

KYOKO?
NOK NOK
YES?
SORRY I'M LATE.
BUT HERE'S THE RENT.
THANKS.
'SCUSE ME.
UM...
YUSAKU?
YEAH?
... ...
WHAT IS IT?
UM...
IT'S NOT IMPOR-TANT.
OKAY, WHAT-EVER.
SEE YOU.
... ...
BOY, WAS HE COLD!

 I TURNED DOWN A FREE MEAL!

 ... ...

 IT IS *NOT!*

IT'S BECAUSE OF THE WAY YOU TREAT HIM.

 MAYBE I'LL TAKE THAT LOAN FROM MY FRIEND.

grrrowl

OH, WELL.

 AS OF TOMOR-ROW, MY FOOD BUDGET IS...

MAYBE I SHOULD HAVE ASKED FOR A DELAY ON THE RENT.

 ... ...

 I'M STARV-ING!

CAN HE REALLY BE THAT UPSET WITH ME?

 HE LOOKS MISER-ABLE.

 GOOD MORNING.

SEE YA.

42

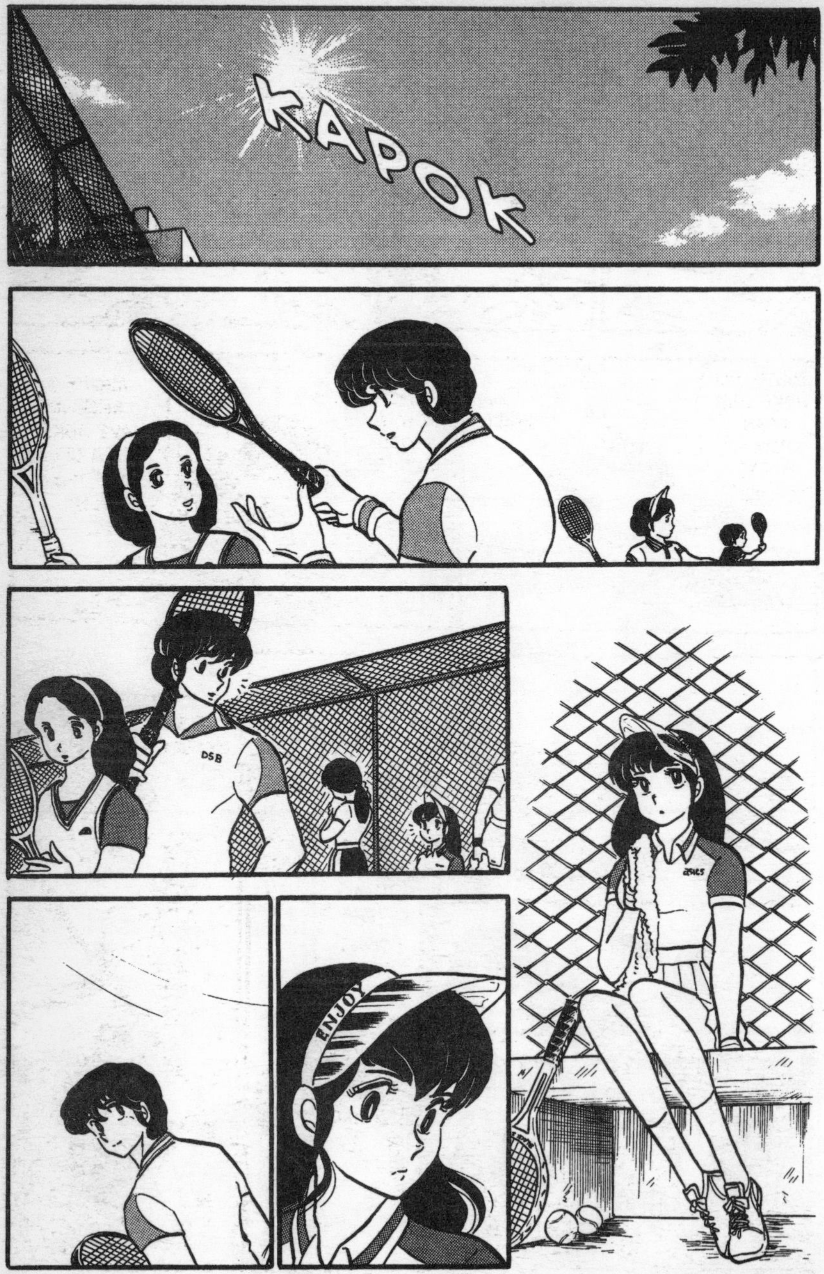
KAPOK
DSB
ENJOY

AKEMI?

HI THERE.

WELL, HI KYOKO!

OH, YEAH, YOU'RE GIVING UP MEN.

WELL... NO!

UH-HUH.

YOU GOT A DATE?

IS THIS YOUR DAY OFF?

THAT'S WHAT I SAID.

I'M DOING NOTHING OF THE KIND.

WELL, AREN'T YOU?

COULD YOU PLEASE NOT PUT IT QUITE THAT WAY?

DON'T WORRY ABOUT IT. I KNOW WHAT YOU MEAN.

I DON'T MEAN I'M NOT... I MEAN...

44

WHY DO YOU SOUND SO HAPPY?

OH! YOU'RE HAVING A FIGHT!

SO, NO MORE DATES WITH THE TENNIS COACH, HUH?

NONE! I HARDLY EVEN SPEAK TO HIM.

BECAUSE I *AM*!

NOT REALLY. HE DOESN'T TRY TO TALK TO ME EITHER.

ISN'T IT KINDA AWKWARD?

I GO THERE TO BRUSH UP ON MY TENNIS, NOT TO SEE SHUN!

THEN WHY DO YOU STILL GO TO THE COURTS?

I SUPPOSE... I WONDER...

CAN IT BE?

...

SO HE DOESN'T LIKE YOU ANYMORE!

45

BUT I'M NOT TRYING TO TIE THEM DOWN!

THE WAY YOU WON'T LET THOSE GUYS GET ANYWHERE BUT YOU STILL TRY TO TIE 'EM DOWN.

IF YOU MUST KNOW, I THINK YOU'RE BEING SELFISH.

YOU... YOU DO?

PLAYING MISS INNOCENT.

THAT'S EVEN SCARIER. DOING IT WITHOUT TRYING!

AKEMI, WOULD YOU *PLEASE* NOT PUT IT THAT WAY!

HE'S GOT TO. HE'S NOT GETTING ANYTHING OFF YOU.

MAYBE HE HAS ANOTHER WOMAN IN HIS LIFE.

POOR SHUN! IN THE PRIME OF HIS MANHOOD, YET!

I'D GIVE HIM WHAT HE NEEDS!

WHY ALL THIS FUSS ABOUT SHUN AND YUSAKU?

SO WHAT IF I'VE BEEN A LITTLE COOL TO THEM?

46

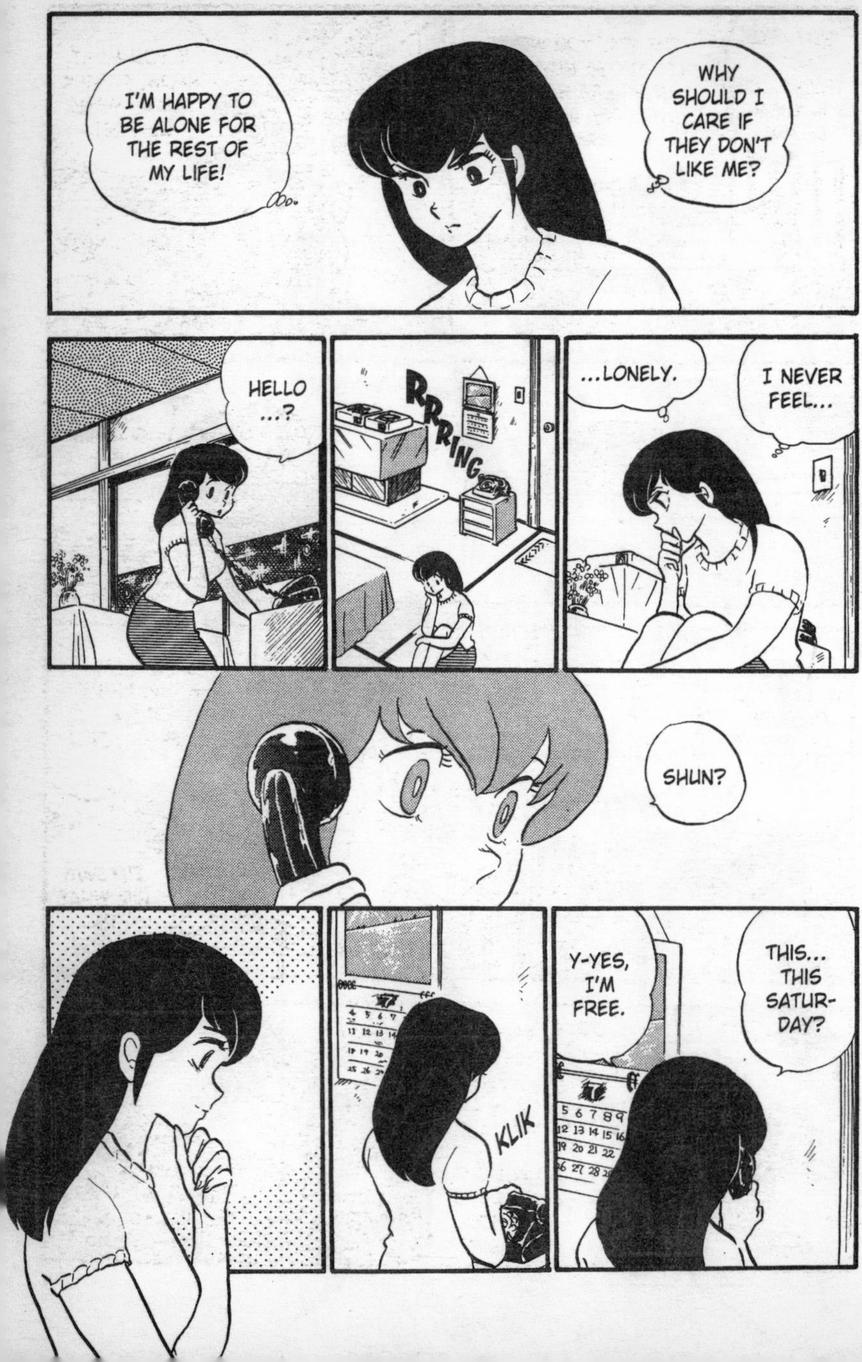
WHY SHOULD I CARE IF THEY DON'T LIKE ME?
I'M HAPPY TO BE ALONE FOR THE REST OF MY LIFE!
I NEVER FEEL...
...LONELY.
RRRING
HELLO ...?
SHUN?
THIS... THIS SATUR-DAY?
Y-YES, I'M FREE.
KLIK

SLIPPIN' THE BUCKS RIGHT INTO MY ACCOUNT!

I CAN EAT AGAIN!

THANK GOD FOR PARENTS!

GREAT TO BE BACK!

WELCOME HOME!

IT'S SO NICE TO SEE A SMILE ON THAT FACE AGAIN!

AND SO THE TRIANGLE IS REPAIRED...

heh heh

heh heh

PART THREE
SOICHIRO TURNS AROUND

BY THE WAY...

THAT'S CORRECT! SO THE SPEAKER IS...

SO THE WORD "INCIDENTALLY" MEANS WHAT?

BY THE WAY...

BY THE WAY...

CORRECT! SO THE SPEAKER IS CHANGING THE SUBJECT.

YOUR FINALS START TOMORROW, RIGHT?

YOU'RE THE ONE CHANGING THE SUBJECT!

WOULD YOU STOP CHANGING THE SUBJECT?!

NOW THIS NEXT PART...

I SAID THAT'S CORRECT!

MY GRANDPA.

WHO TOLD YOU THAT?!

IS IT TRUE AUNTIE KYOKO'S GETTING REMARRIED?

TOK

UM...

IF THE SPEAKER'S CHANGING THE...

TO *WHOM*?!

I HOPE IT'S OKAY!

I'M OPENING THE DOOR!

H-HERE I AM!

SO IF HE'S CHANGING THE SUBJECT...

I GET IT.

NOK NOK

WHO'S SHE SUPPOSED TO BE MARRYING?!

DON'T CHANGE THE SUBJECT!

ANSWER ME, IKUKO!

I'M COMING IN!

51

KLOP
KLOP
KLOP
KLIK

ARE YOU PAYING ATTENTION, IKUKO?

I AM!

SINCE YUSAKU'S SPENDING THIS EXTRA TIME...

OKAY, GRANDPA WAS SAYING...

SO WHAT ABOUT HER REMARRYING, HUH?

...THEN SHE WON'T BE UNCLE SOICHIRO'S WIFE ANYMORE...

IF AUNTIE KYOKO GETS REMARRIED...

...HOW MAYBE IT'S TIME SHE GETS MARRIED AGAIN. 'CAUSE HE'S GETTING WORRIED ABOUT HER.

WHAT WOULD SHE BE THEN?

...SO SHE WON'T BE ABLE TO BE MY AUNT!

THE WORD'S "UN-RELATED."

OH, JEEZ.

IS THAT ALL?

52

HOW COME?

I DON'T THINK YOU'VE GOTTA WORRY...

...MUCH.

...

...

I DON'T WANT THAT TO HAPPEN.

GREAT!

I THINK IT'LL BE A WHILE.

WELL...

WHEN YOU LIVE IN THE SAME BUILDING, YOU GET TO KNOW PEOPLE.

AUNTIE...

DID YOU GET ALL YOUR QUESTIONS ANSWERED?

UH-HUH.

WHAT?

DO YOU STILL REMEMBER THINGS ABOUT UNCLE SOICHIRO?

...RIGHT HERE IN MY CHEST...

IT USED TO BE, WHENEVER I THOUGHT OF HIM...

BUT SOMEHOW... IT DOESN'T HURT MUCH ANYMORE.

?

YES. I REMEMBER.

YOU KNOW, I'VE ALWAYS WANTED TO ASK YOU...

...IT WAS PHYSICALLY PAINFUL.

WOW...

...IT WOULD BECOME SO TIGHT...

IT JUST HAPPENED.

WHY DID YOU GIVE UNCLE SOICHIRO'S NAME TO THE DOG?

54

HM?

OH, SOICHIRO!

HE'S FILTHY. HE MUST BE A STRAY.

HE FOLLOWED ME FROM THE STATION.

WHO'S THE DOG?

55

JUST IGNORE HIM.

HE ISN'T GOING AWAY AS IT IS!

SOONER OR LATER HE'LL LEAVE.

SHOULD I GIVE HIM SOME?

I GUESS HE WANTS MY YAKITORI.

IF YOU DO THAT, HE'LL NEVER GO AWAY!

THAT'S YOUR NAME, DON'T YOU UNDERSTAND?

SNOWY.

BOY, YOU'VE GOT SOME NERVE FOR A DOG!

AND HE'S BEEN HERE EVER SINCE.

BOWF!

OKAY.

DINNER'S READY, SOICHIRO.

SNOWY!

...
...

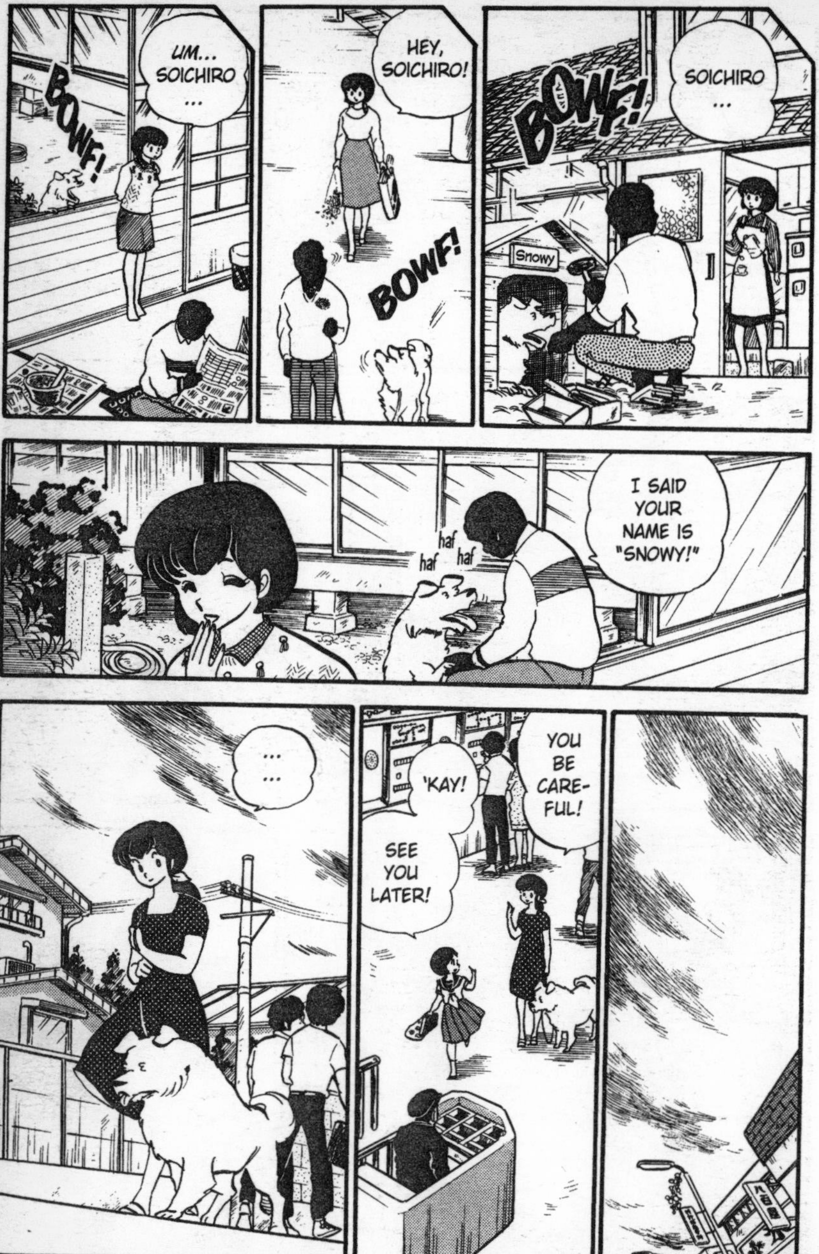
UM... SOICHIRO ...
BOWF!
HEY, SOICHIRO!
BOWF!
BOWF!
SOICHIRO ...
Snowy
haf haf haf
I SAID YOUR NAME IS "SNOWY!"
... ...
'KAY!
SEE YOU LATER!
YOU BE CAREFUL!

IS MR. SOICHIRO BACK?

WHAT'S WRONG, KENTARO?

A FEW DAYS LATER.

MISS MANAGER!

WELL... UH... SEE...

BUT YOU WERE THE ONE WHO TOOK HIM FOR A WALK!

WHEN I WAS AT THE RAILROAD CROSSING...

...

HE GOT LOST!

DING DING DING

MR. SOICHIRO! STOP!

snf snf

DING DING DING

Sniffff

58

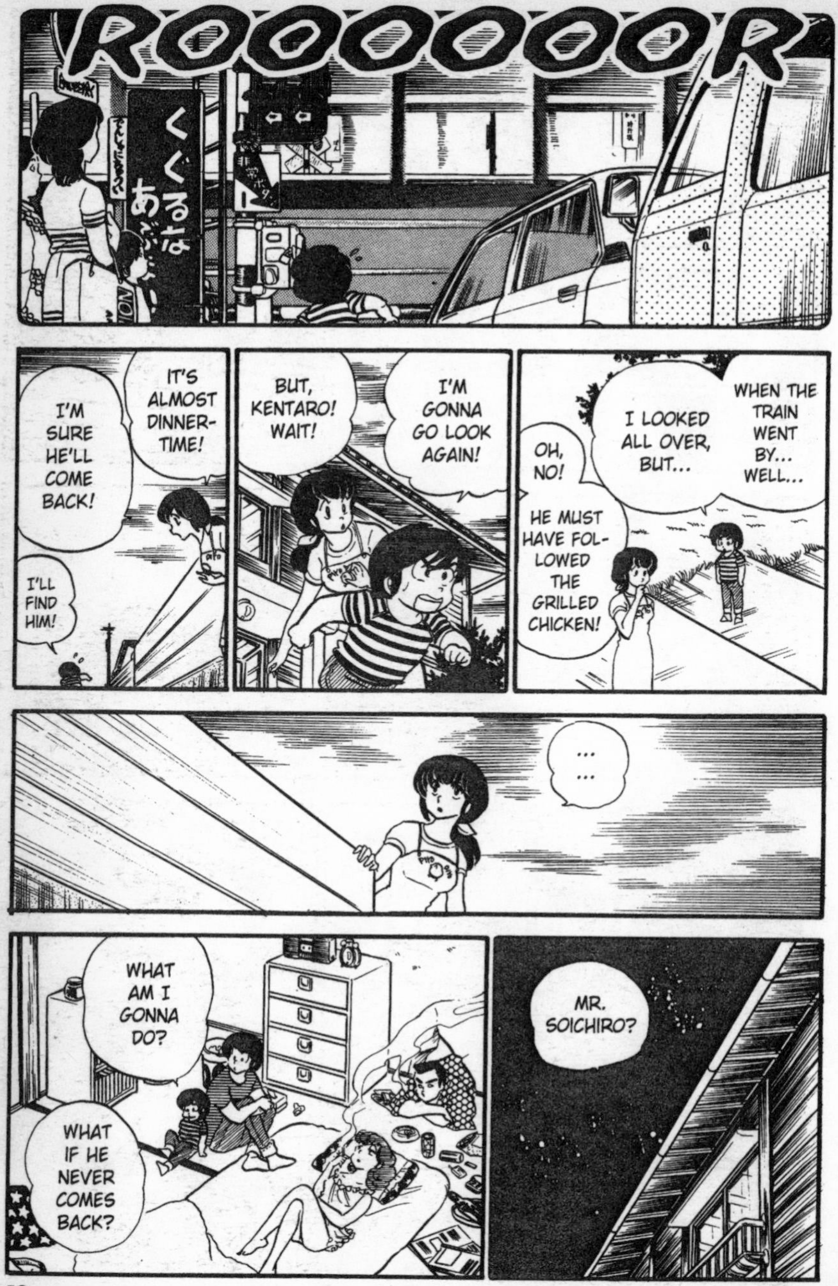
ROOOOOOR
WHEN THE TRAIN WENT BY... WELL...
I LOOKED ALL OVER, BUT...
OH, NO!
HE MUST HAVE FOL-LOWED THE GRILLED CHICKEN!
I'M GONNA GO LOOK AGAIN!
BUT, KENTARO! WAIT!
IT'S ALMOST DINNER-TIME!
I'M SURE HE'LL COME BACK!
I'LL FIND HIM!
... ...
MR. SOICHIRO?
WHAT AM I GONNA DO?
WHAT IF HE NEVER COMES BACK?

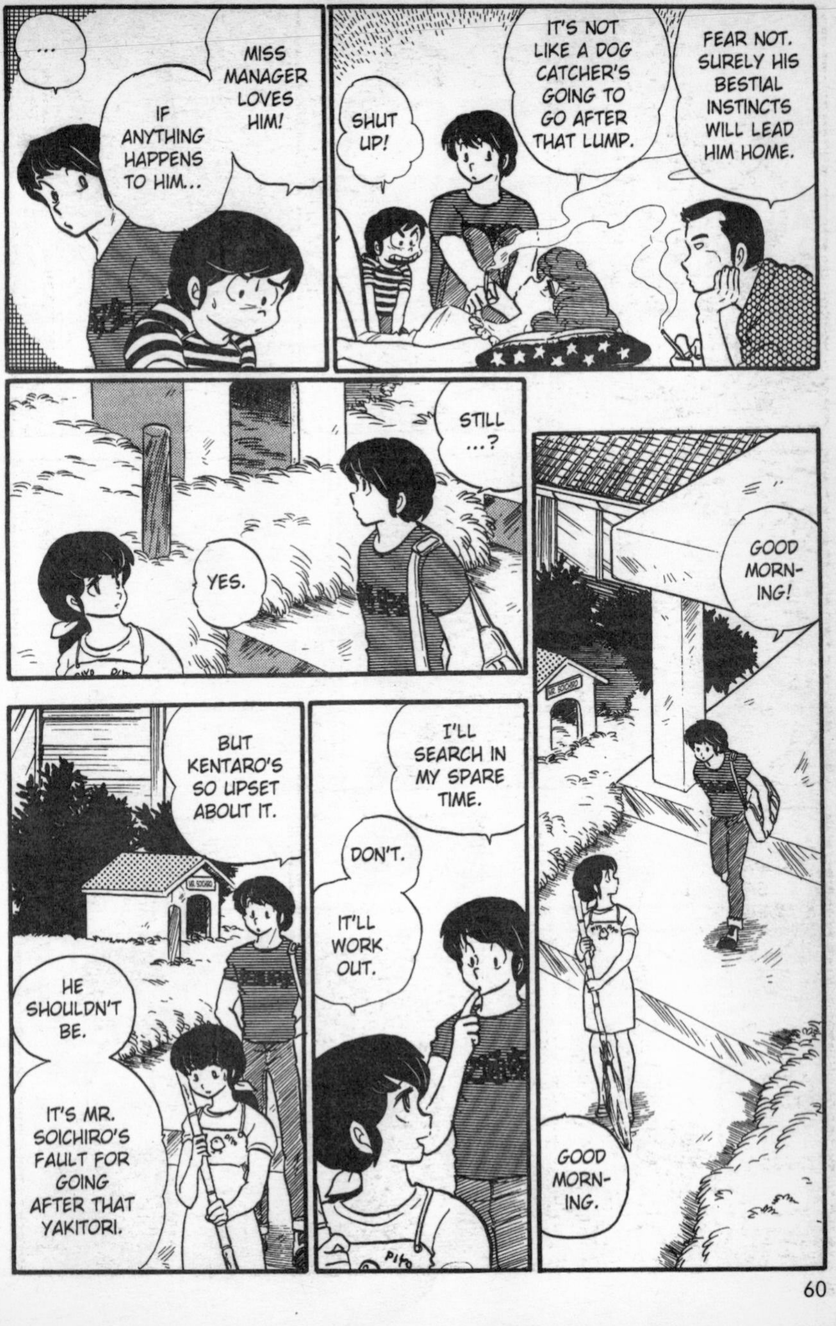
...
MISS MANAGER LOVES HIM!
IF ANYTHING HAPPENS TO HIM...
SHUT UP!
IT'S NOT LIKE A DOG CATCHER'S GOING TO GO AFTER THAT LUMP.
FEAR NOT. SURELY HIS BESTIAL INSTINCTS WILL LEAD HIM HOME.
GOOD MORNING!
GOOD MORNING.
STILL ...?
YES.
BUT KENTARO'S SO UPSET ABOUT IT.
HE SHOULDN'T BE.
IT'S MR. SOICHIRO'S FAULT FOR GOING AFTER THAT YAKITORI.
I'LL SEARCH IN MY SPARE TIME.
DON'T.
IT'LL WORK OUT.

OH!

LOST DOG

OLD MANGY WHITE DOG CALL (04

LOST DOG

OLD MANGY WHITE DOG CALL

...

...

...DID HE HAVE TO SAY "MANGY"?

BUT...

I ALWAYS THOUGHT OF HIM AS "SHAGGY."

HE MUST REALLY FEEL TERRIBLE.

LOST DOG

OLD MANGY WHITE DOG CALL

OH, KEN-TARO...

A WEEK PASSES.

SUDDENLY IT FEELS HUGE.

ALWAYS THOUGHT THIS WAS A SMALL TOWN.

A BIG OLD WHITE MANGY ONE?

UH-UH! SORRY!

HEY, KIDS, HAVE YOU SEEN A STRAY DOG AROUND?

IT'S ALL RIGHT, REALLY.

PLEASE TELL POOR KENTARO NOT TO FEEL BAD.

MY KID'S SO DAMN CARELESS.

I'M REALLY SORRY.

WE'RE ALL SO WORRIED.

WHERE CAN YOU BE?

GUESS I'LL CHECK THE POUND AGAIN.

BUT I'M RUNNING OUT OF HOPE.

...
...

HEY, LOOK! A DEAD DOG!

WHERE?

MUST'VE GOT HIT BY A CAR!

POOR DOG.

MR. SOICHIRO

IT'S NOT HIM.

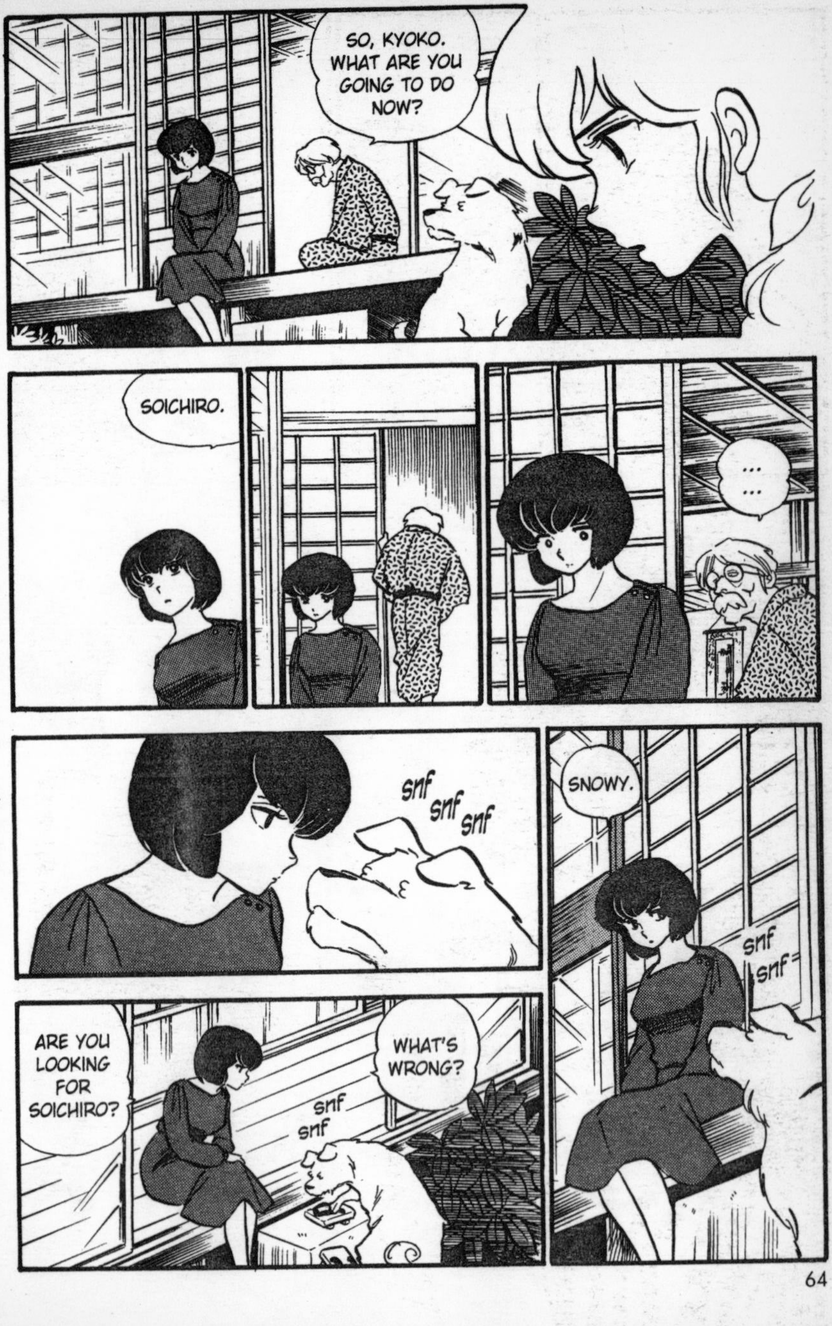
SO, KYOKO. WHAT ARE YOU GOING TO DO NOW?
SOICHIRO.
...
...
snf snf snf
SNOWY.
snf snf
WHAT'S WRONG?
ARE YOU LOOKING FOR SOICHIRO?
snf snf

...
...

snf snf snf

...GONE. HE'S...

SOICHIRO ISN'T HERE ANYMORE.

OH, SOICHIRO...

HE WANTS TO NAME IT...

BUT MOM!

WOULD YOU TWO BE QUIET?!

NO, IT'S NOT! IT'S JULIE!

IT'S CAESAR!

WHERE WOULD THAT STUPID DOG GO?

NOT AT THE POUND...

"DOPEY" IS THE NAME FOR THAT MUTT!

QUIET! YOU CAN'T CALL A MANGY DOG LIKE THAT CAESAR OR JULIE!

HE BARKED 'CAUSE YOU GAVE HIM FOOD!

YOU SEE? HE BARKED WHEN I CALLED HIM DOPEY!

BOWF

SOICHIRO!

HERE'S YOUR DINNER, DOPEY!

BOWF

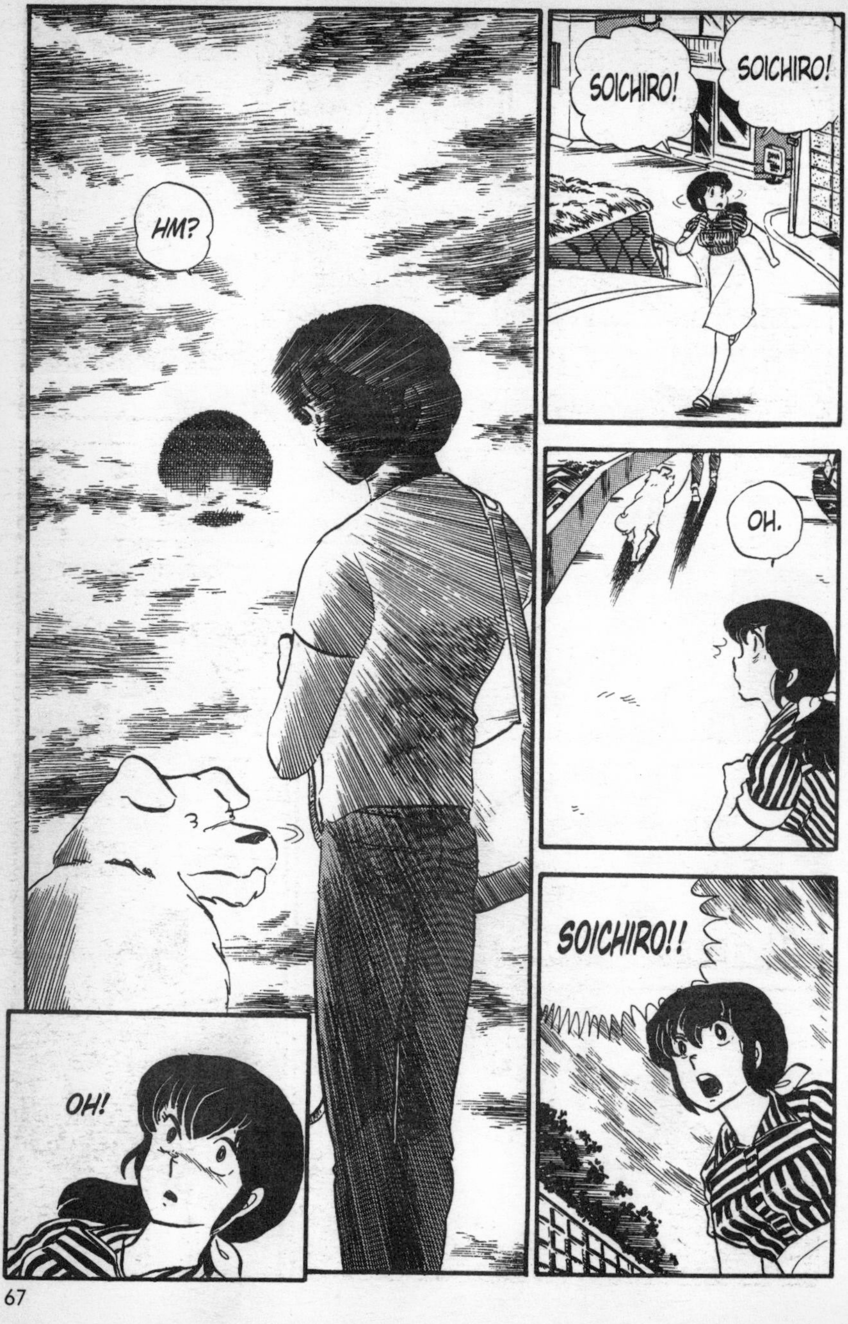
SOICHIRO!
SOICHIRO!
OH.
SOICHIRO!!
HM?
OH!

AREN'T YOU HAPPY, KYOKO?

...

haf haf

GO GET HER, SOICHIRO!

BOWf

...

...

I DON'T GET HER.

I THOUGHT I'D BE MAKING HER HAPPY.

THE STRANGEST THING.

BUT YUSAKU LOOKS NOTHING LIKE HIM.

IS SOMETHING WRONG?

UM... KYOKO?

WHAT?

THANK YOU VERY MUCH.

OH! UM...

68

PART FOUR
A BUNCH OF MUGS

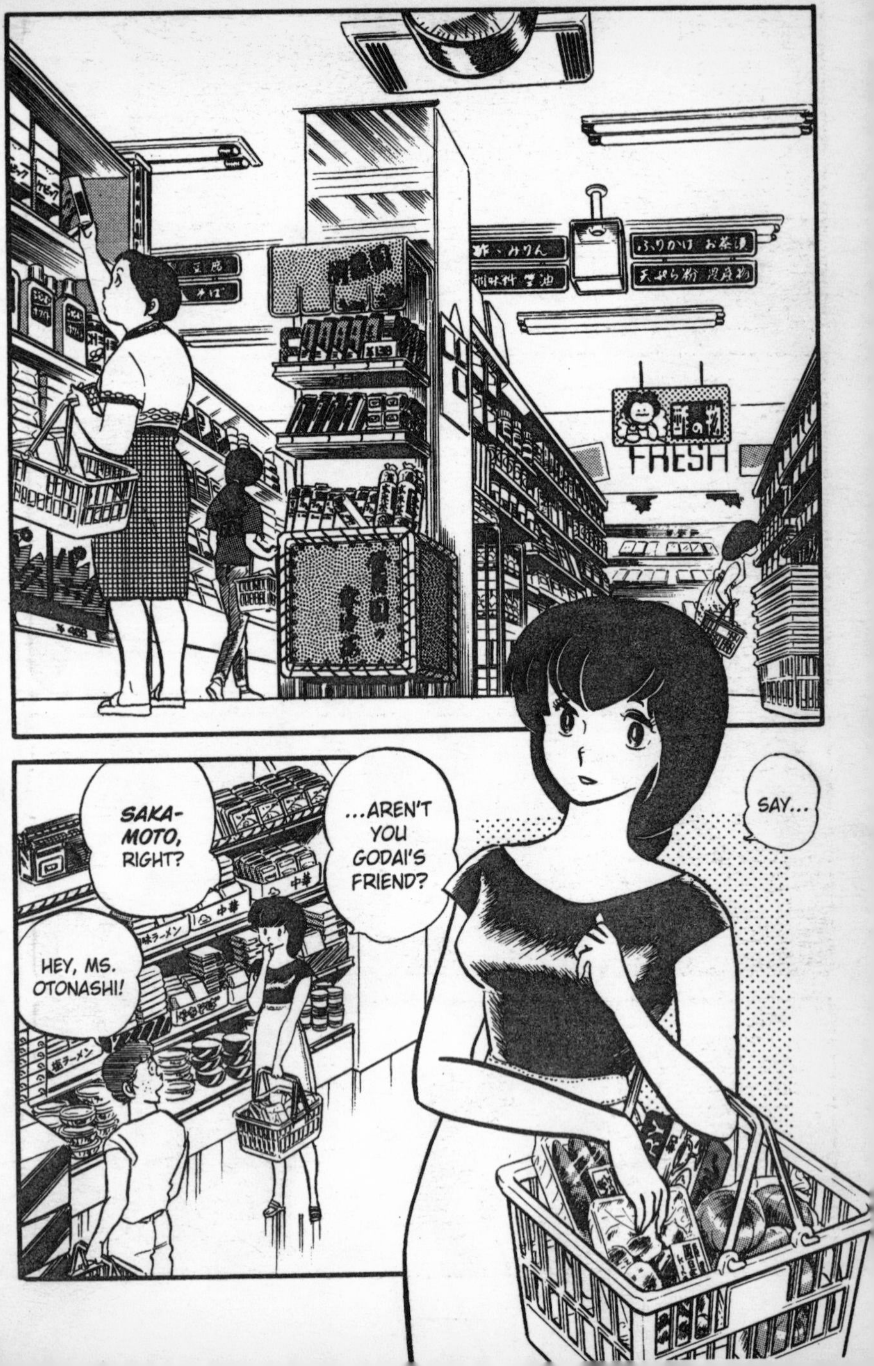
FRESH
SAY...
...AREN'T YOU GODAI'S FRIEND?
SAKA-MOTO, RIGHT?
HEY, MS. OTONASHI!

WELL, I GOT THIS JOB AT A PUB—

ARE YOU IN THE AREA TO VISIT HIM?

GOOD IDEA.

IT'S ONLY FOR A WEEK OR SO, SO I FIGURED I'D JUST CAMP OUT AT HIS PLACE.

YEAH... THE BIG ONE ACROSS FROM THE STATION.

THE ONE YUSAKU'S WORKING AT?

NAW, IT'S THE WHOLE WEEK'S WORTH.

YOU MUST BE HUNGRY...

BUYING DINNER?

YUP.

WELL, I FIGURE I'LL GRAB A BITE OUT, EVERY ONCE IN A WHILE.

THAT'S NOT MUCH, THEN.

SAKAMOTO, MA'AM.

YUSAKU'S FRIEND FROM COLLEGE...

SAY... YOU'RE... UM...

YES?

KYOKO, I'M—

NOT MUCH...

SO WHAT WERE YOU TALKING ABOUT?

YOU BET!

SEE YOU BACK AT THE APARTMENT.

THE GYOZA THEY MAKE HERE ARE GREAT — LOADED WITH GARLIC!

HEY, SAKAMOTO, WANNA GRAB SOME POT STICKERS?

MAN, WHAT A LADY...

WHAT ?!

I FINALLY GOT TO TALK TO YOUR APARTMENT MANAGER...

WHAT'S YOUR PROBLEM?

WELL, *THAT* BROUGHT ME BACK TO EARTH...

WHAT ARE YOU COMPLAINING ABOUT? YOU *LIVE* WITH HER!

YOU MORON! WHY DIDN'T YOU CALL ME?!

IT'S MORE LIKE TORTURE.

YOU REALLY THINK SO?

LUCKY SLOB...

MAN, YOU LUCKY SLOB...

HAVING A BABE LIKE THAT AROUND ALL THE TIME...

JUST 'CAUSE SHE'S NEAR DOESN'T—

A "WORM"?!

NOT EXACTLY!

KINDA LIKE HAVING A WORM ON A HOOK IN FRONT OF YOU ALL THE TIME?

...
...

THE BUSTED ONES ARE YOURS.

...AND I HAVE TO RESIST THE SUDDEN URGE TO GRAB HER AND SQUEEZE HER TIGHT.

KRUNCH

WHEN WE TALK, STANDING CLOSE... THE AIR IS FILLED WITH HER HEAVENLY SCENT...

NICE TO SEE YOU AGAIN, MA'AM.

HELLO, BOYS.

WE'RE HOME!

HUH?

DO YOU LIKE CURRY, SAKA-MOTO?

WOULD I? YOU GOTTA BE KIDDIN'!

I GOT CARRIED AWAY COOKING UP SOME FOR DINNER AND MADE TOO MUCH — WOULD YOU CARE TO JOIN ME?

...GIVE ME ABOUT A HALF-HOUR.

WELL...

YEAH, OKAY...

OF COURSE YOU'RE WELCOME, TOO, YUSAKU.

YES'M!

74

MAN, YOU'RE LUCKY... SHE'S SO NICE.

"YOU'RE WELCOME, *TOO*," SHE SAYS...

WHAT DOES THAT MEAN, "TOO"...?

WHAT'S UP, YUSAKU?

"NICE," HUH... THAT REMINDS ME...

GREAT, GREAT!

HOW IS IT, YUSAKU?

SEEMS LIKE IT'S BEEN A LONG TIME SINCE SHE'S BEEN SO NICE TO *ME*...

IF *YOU* WEREN'T HERE, I'D AGREE!

HA HA HA

JUST "GREAT"...? IT'S THE BEST I'VE EVER HAD!

THE *DEATH* PART CAN BE ARRANGED...

GEE, YUSAKU... SOMETHING WRONG?

DAMN YOU, SAKAMOTO!

MAN, I'D *DIE* TO HAVE A WIFE LIKE YOU, KYOKO!

OH, COME ON!

WELL, HEY, THEN YOU GOTTA COME TO THE PUB!

WELL, A LITTLE BIT'S OKAY...

YOU MEAN LIQUOR?

SAY, MA'AM... YOU A DRINKER AT ALL?

OH, DON'T WORRY...

ER... I'LL PAY AS THANKS FOR DINNER.

OH, C'MON... I INSIST.

YOU DON'T OWE ME ANY-THING.

76

YOU COOKED DINNER FOR MY FRIEND HERE, SO NOW I OWE YOU ONE.

WELL...

I MEAN, THIS IS REALLY BETWEEN YOU AND ME, RIGHT?

OH, NO, HE WON'T! IT'S MINE!

DON'T FORGET! AND I'LL PICK UP THE TAB.

MAYBE I'LL DROP BY TOMORROW, OKAY?

...

...

I JUST DON'T LIKE GUYS MAKING PASSES AT MY MANAGER!

YOU ACT LIKE YOU OWN HER!

JEEZ...

YOU EXPECT ME TO SWALLOW THAT OLD LINE?

AIN'T YOU EVER HEARD OF ADMIRING SOMEONE FROM AFAR?

DON'T GIVE ME THAT CRAP, YOU LECH.

AW, C'MON... I WAS JUST BEING NICE TO HER.

AIEE!

POOR YUSAKU'S DESIRE REMAINS UNREQUITED.

ZHOOP

FORGET IT — THERE'S ONLY ENOUGH FOR THE TWO OF US.

HAVING A FEW DRINKS? HOW NICE.

JEEZ, I THOUGHT YOU WERE SOME KINDA SNAKE-MAN OR SOMETHIN'...

UH, HI....

GOOD EVENING. I AM YOTSUYA.

I SHALL SOMEHOW ENDURE.

GOOD!

I SEE...

ABSOLUTELY.

ARE YOU CERTAIN?

78

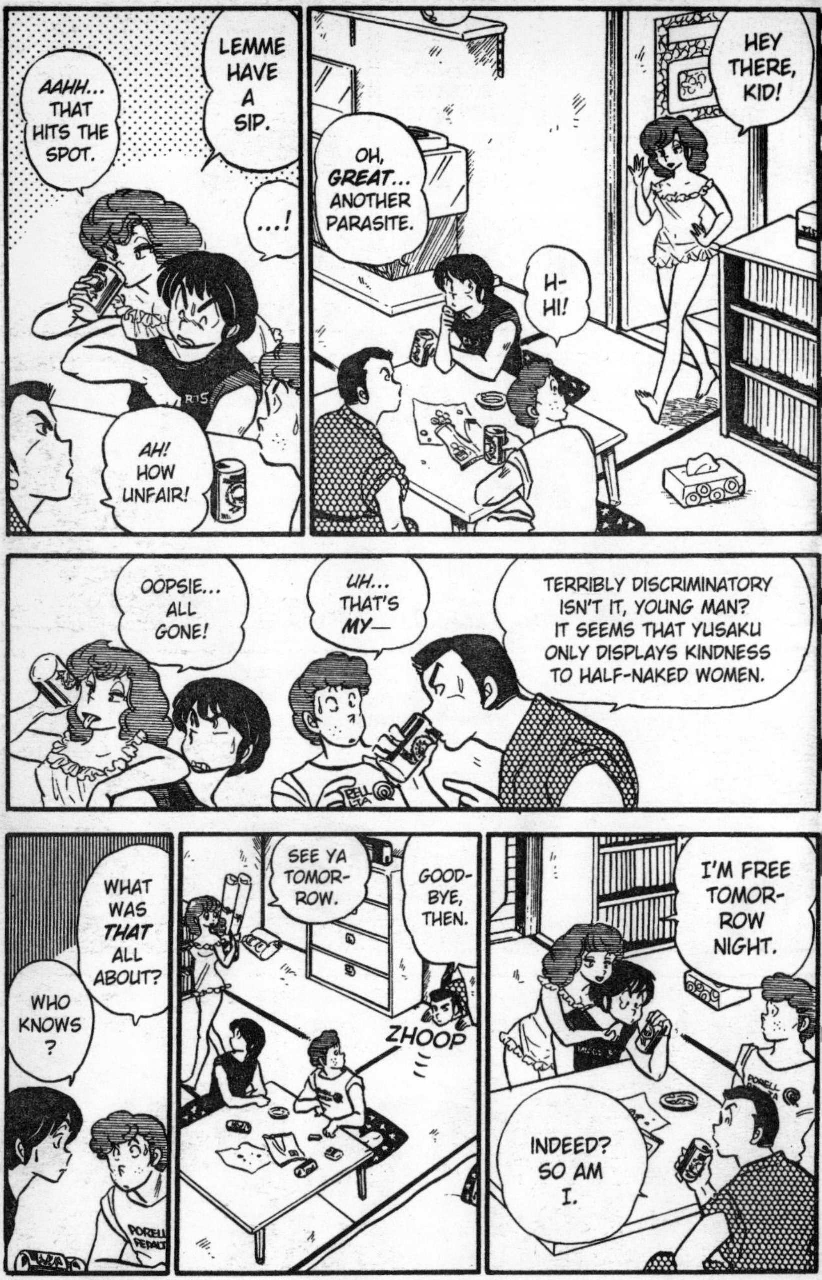
AAHH... THAT HITS THE SPOT.
LEMME HAVE A SIP.
...!
AH! HOW UNFAIR!
HEY THERE, KID!
OH, GREAT... ANOTHER PARASITE.
H- HI!
OOPSIE... ALL GONE!
UH... THAT'S MY—
TERRIBLY DISCRIMINATORY ISN'T IT, YOUNG MAN? IT SEEMS THAT YUSAKU ONLY DISPLAYS KINDNESS TO HALF-NAKED WOMEN.
WHAT WAS THAT ALL ABOUT?
WHO KNOWS ?
SEE YA TOMOR-ROW.
GOOD-BYE, THEN.
ZHOOP
I'M FREE TOMOR-ROW NIGHT.
INDEED? SO AM I.

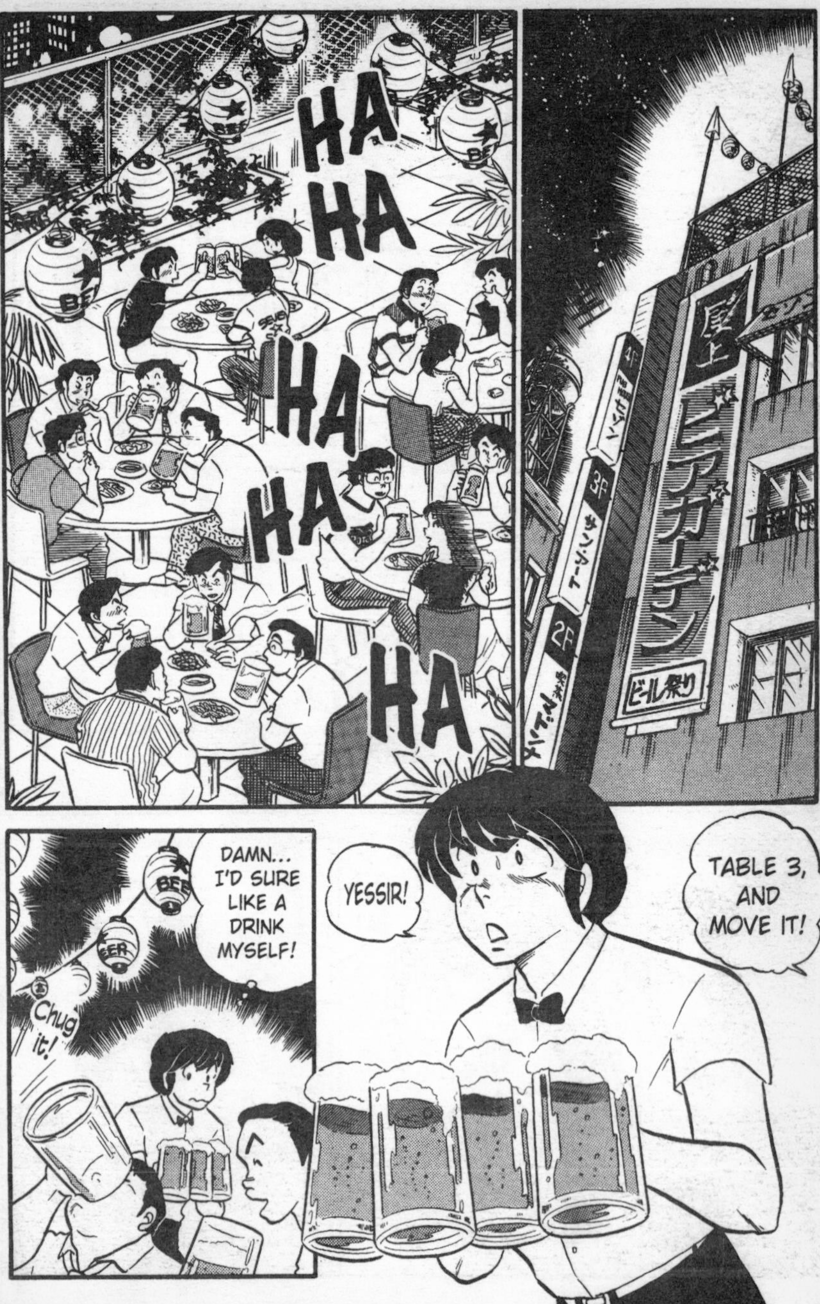
HA
HA
HA
HA
HA
屋上ビアガーデン
ビール祭り
3F
サン・アート
2F
4F
TABLE 3, AND MOVE IT!
YESSIR!
Chug it!
DAMN... I'D SURE LIKE A DRINK MYSELF!

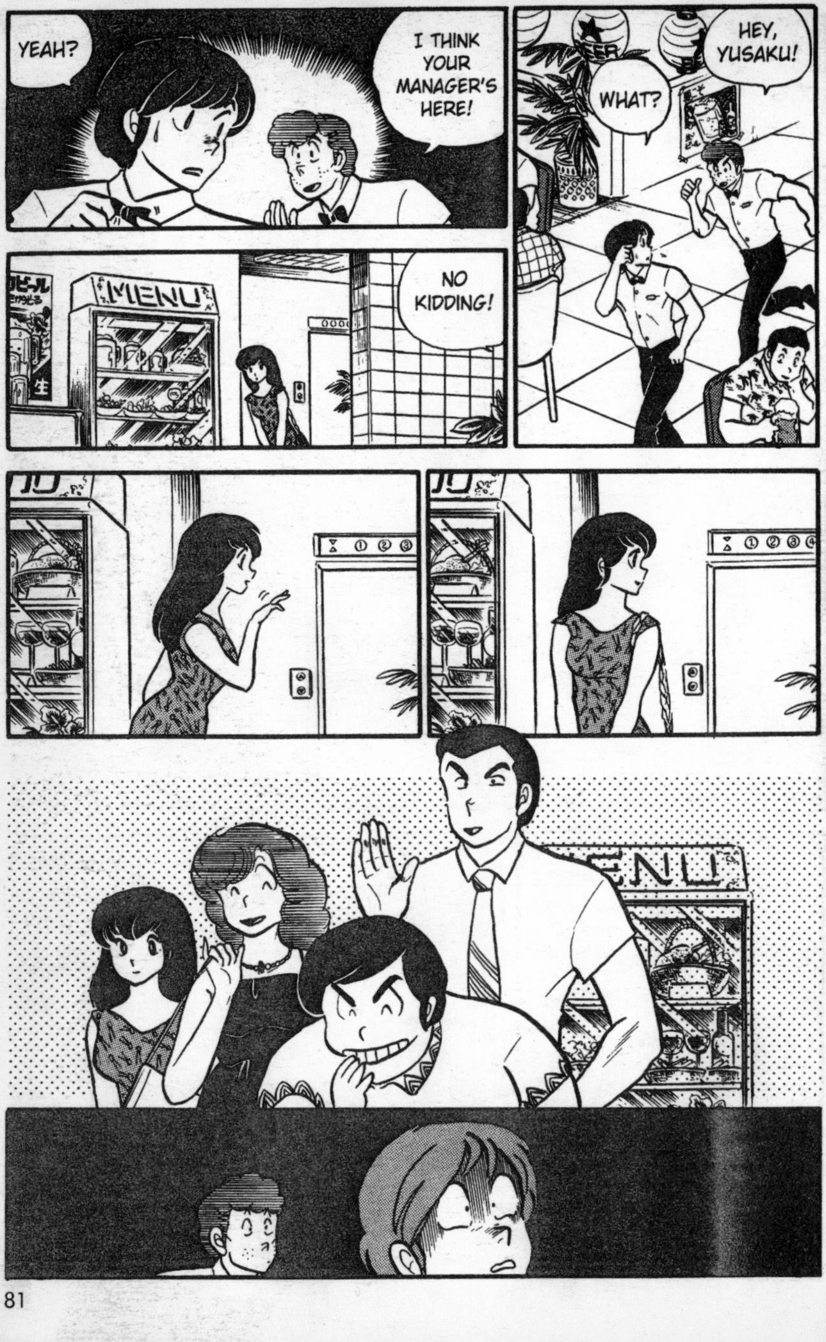
HEY, YUSAKU!
WHAT?
I THINK YOUR MANAGER'S HERE!
YEAH?
NO KIDDING!
MENU
MENU

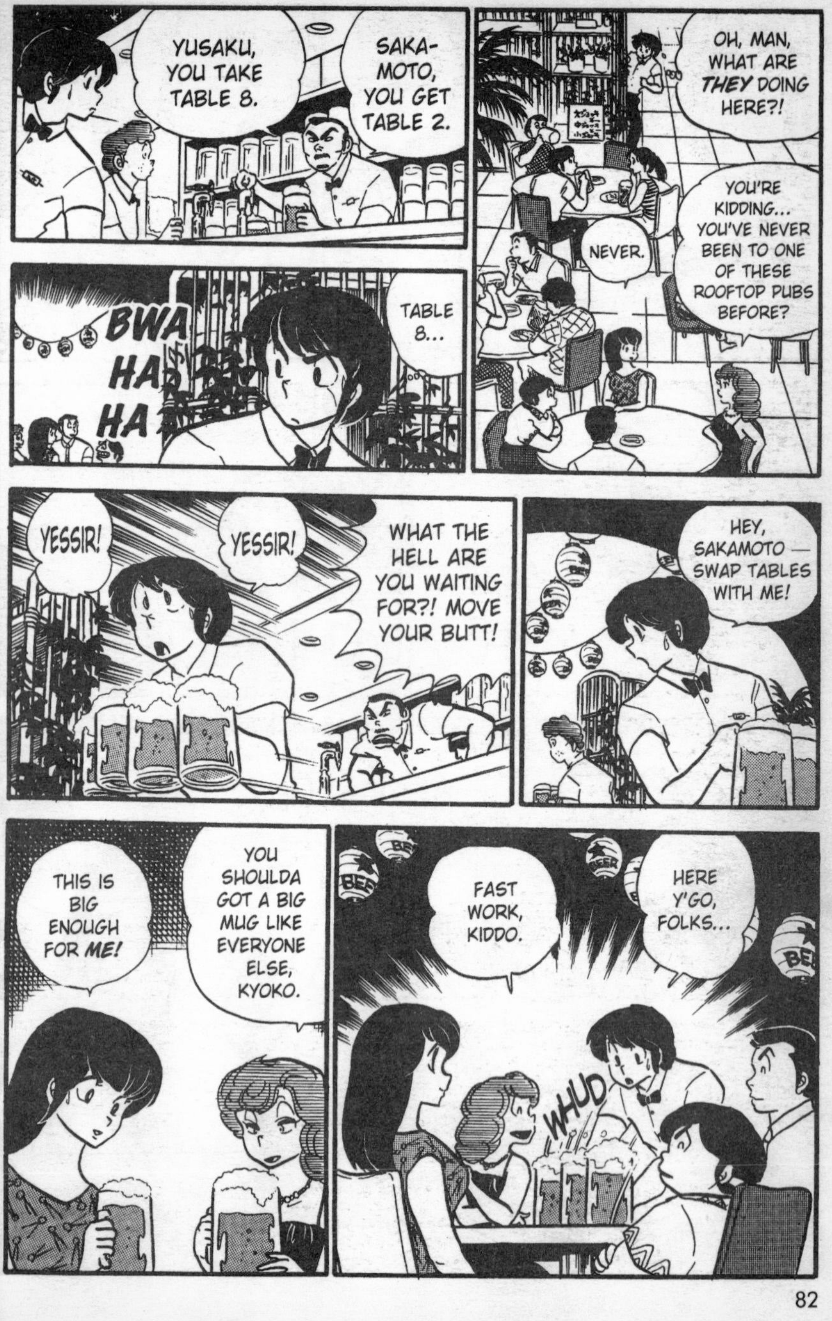

YUSAKU, YOU TAKE TABLE 8.
SAKA-MOTO, YOU GET TABLE 2.
BWA HA HA
TABLE 8...
OH, MAN, WHAT ARE *THEY* DOING HERE?!
YOU'RE KIDDING... YOU'VE NEVER BEEN TO ONE OF THESE ROOFTOP PUBS BEFORE?
NEVER.
YESSIR!
YESSIR!
WHAT THE HELL ARE YOU WAITING FOR?! MOVE YOUR BUTT!
HEY, SAKAMOTO — SWAP TABLES WITH ME!
THIS IS BIG ENOUGH FOR *ME!*
YOU SHOULDA GOT A BIG MUG LIKE EVERYONE ELSE, KYOKO.
FAST WORK, KIDDO.
HERE Y'GO, FOLKS...
WHUD

EXCUSE ME...?

....!

MOST KIND OF YOU TO INVITE US TO SHARE IN YOUR GOOD FORTUNE.

YEAH, YUSAKU'S PAYING ANYWAY, RIGHT?

...

...

LET'S HEAR IT FOR YU-SAKU!

CHEERS!

HEY, WAIT A SEC! WHO INVITED WHOM FOR WHAT?!

I'M SURE I DON'T KNOW.

SUCK IT UP, GUYS — IT'S ALL FREE!

BETTER KEEP 'EM COMING *FAST!*

WE ACCEPT YOUR KIND OFFER.

HI GUYS! DRINK UP, DRINK UP – YUSAKU'LL KEEP 'EM COMING!

HONESTLY, I DON'T HAVE A CLUE...

SOMEHOW THINGS JUST GOT ALL MIXED UP.

LOOK, KYOKO... WHAT'S GOING ON HERE?

Y-YESSIR!

DON'T STOP AND YAK WITH THE CUSTOMERS WHEN WE'RE THIS BUSY, YOU KNUCKLEHEAD!

HEY, YUSAKU — THE BOSS WANTS YA!

BWAHAHAHA!

M-ME? NO WAY!

WHAT THE HELL?!

YOU KNOW THEM?

ALL *RIGHT*, LADY!

BWA HA HA HA!

MRS. ICHINOSE, PLEASE!

HEY, YUSAKU! C'MON, FILL 'EM UP!

84

M... MAYBE SHE SAW IT ON MY NAME TAG?

SO HOW COME SHE KNOWS YOUR FIRST NAME?

SEZ WHO?

MAYBE, BUT YOU'RE EMBARRASSING KYOKO!

HA HA

AW, THEY LOVE IT!

C'MON GUYS, CHILL OUT. YOU'RE NOT THE ONLY PEOPLE HERE!

...AND SURE ENOUGH...!

BWA HA HA

I THOUGHT THIS MIGHT HAPPEN...

I AM NOT!

SHE'S JUST DRUNK!

LOOK! SHE'S BLUSHING!

HEE HEE

IF I'M NOT HERE TO KEEP CONTROL, THEY'LL...

BUT I CAN'T JUST GO HOME AND LEAVE YUSAKU STUCK WITH THEM.

Chug it! Chug it!

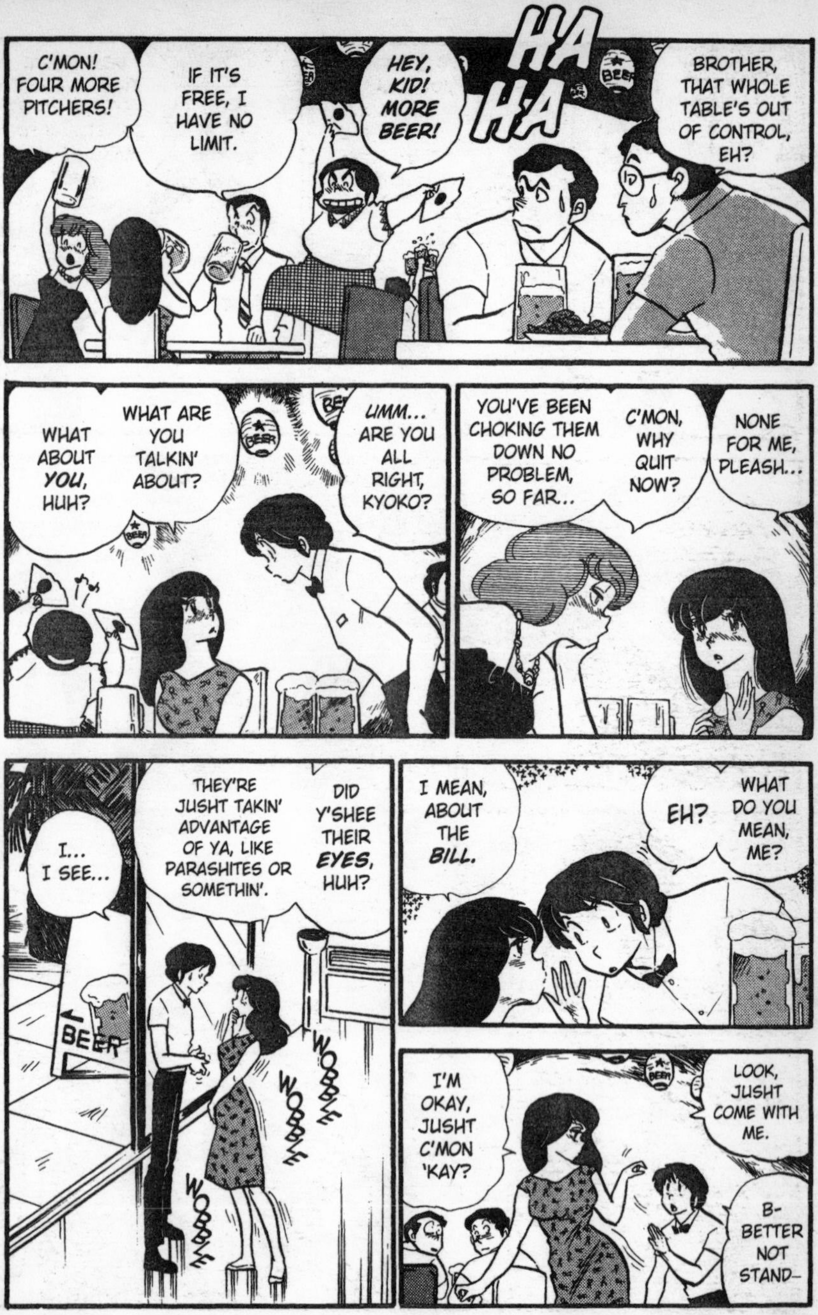
C'MON! FOUR MORE PITCHERS!
IF IT'S FREE, I HAVE NO LIMIT.
HEY, KID! MORE BEER!
HA HA
BEER
BROTHER, THAT WHOLE TABLE'S OUT OF CONTROL, EH?
WHAT ABOUT *YOU*, HUH?
WHAT ARE YOU TALKIN' ABOUT?
UMM... ARE YOU ALL RIGHT, KYOKO?
YOU'VE BEEN CHOKING THEM DOWN NO PROBLEM, SO FAR..
C'MON, WHY QUIT NOW?
NONE FOR ME, PLEASH...
I... I SEE...
THEY'RE JUSHT TAKIN' ADVANTAGE OF YA, LIKE PARASHITES OR SOMETHIN'.
DID Y'SHEE THEIR *EYES*, HUH?
BEER
WOBBLE
WOBBLE
WOBBLE
I MEAN, ABOUT THE *BILL*.
EH?
WHAT DO YOU MEAN, ME?
I'M OKAY, JUSHT C'MON 'KAY?
LOOK, JUSHT COME WITH ME.
B-BETTER NOT STAND-

HUH?!

T'NIGHT, *I'M* GONNA ⊰HIC⊱ PAY.

Y-YES...?

PEOPLE TAKE ADVANTAGE OF YA 'CAUSE YOU'RE SHO INDECISHIVE, HUH?

Y-YES...?

DON' GIMME THAT "I SHEE" STUFF! OOH! SOMETIMSH YOU MAKE ME *SHO MAD!*

YOU THINK *FAIRNESH* OR *MORALSH* MEAN *ANYTHIN'* TO *THOSH* PEOPLE?!

B-BUT THAT'S *NOT FAIR!* YOU'VE GOTTA MAKE THEM CHIP IN!

K-KYOKO!

(ULP!)

UMM... KYOKO... DON'T YOU THINK YOU'RE A LITTLE A DRUNK?

JUSHT LEAVE IT T'—

WHAP

MY "DEAR KYOKO"...?

YOU JUSHT LEAVE IT T' YOUR DEAR KYOKO!

WHAP

WOBBLE

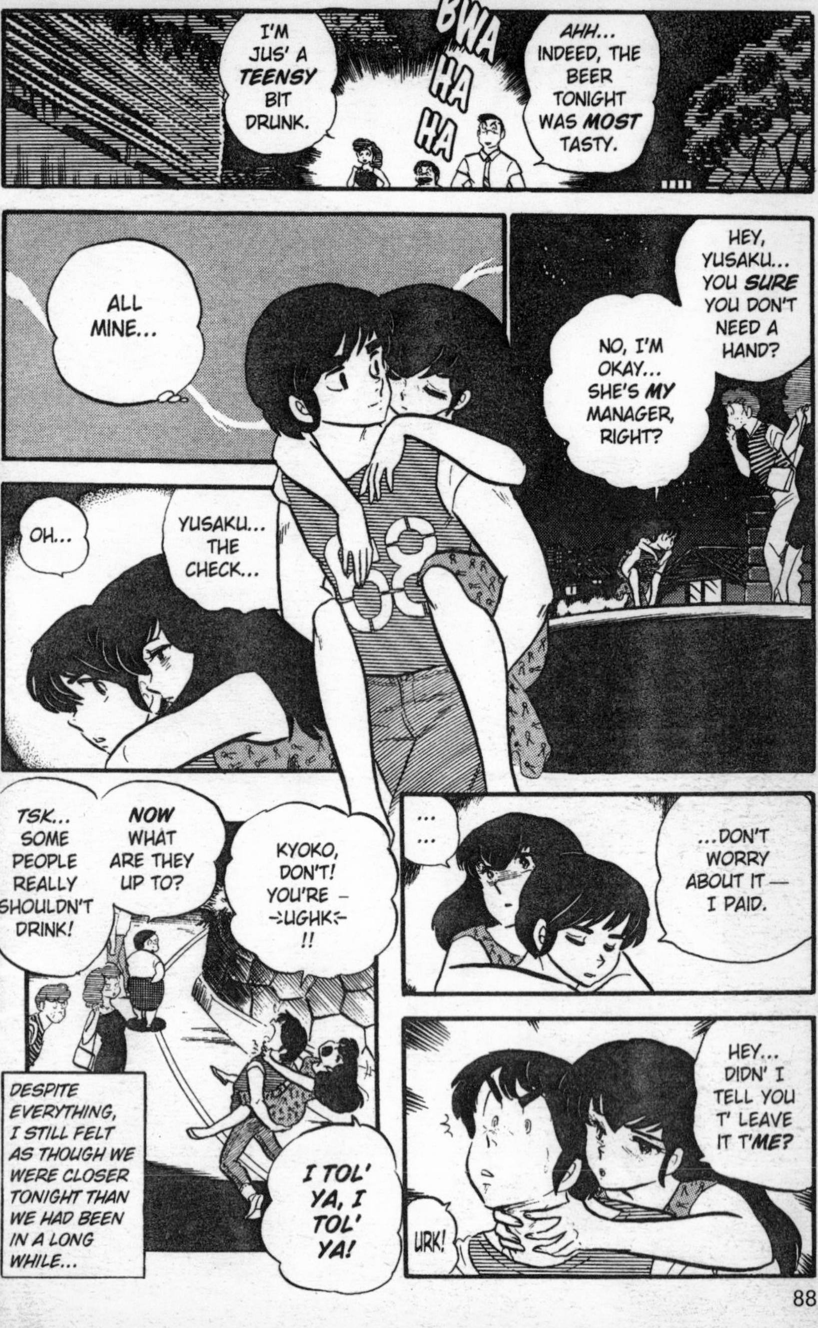
I'M JUS' A TEENSY BIT DRUNK.
BWA HA HA HA
AHH... INDEED, THE BEER TONIGHT WAS MOST TASTY.
ALL MINE...
HEY, YUSAKU... YOU SURE YOU DON'T NEED A HAND?
NO, I'M OKAY... SHE'S MY MANAGER, RIGHT?
OH...
YUSAKU... THE CHECK...
TSK... SOME PEOPLE REALLY SHOULDN'T DRINK!
NOW WHAT ARE THEY UP TO?
KYOKO, DON'T! YOU'RE — UGHK !!
DESPITE EVERYTHING, I STILL FELT AS THOUGH WE WERE CLOSER TONIGHT THAN WE HAD BEEN IN A LONG WHILE...
I TOL' YA, I TOL' YA!
... ...
...DON'T WORRY ABOUT IT — I PAID.
HEY... DIDN' I TELL YOU T' LEAVE IT T'ME?
URK!

PART FIVE
THE ONE THAT GOT AWAY

SUMMER
AMUSEMENTS;
BUT THE ONE THAT
GOT AWAY;
BREAKS MORE
THAN A NET.

A FESTIVAL, HUH...

BAM BAM BAM BAM

THEY MUST BE PUTTING ON FESTIVALS BACK IN MY HOMETOWN, TOO...

DON'T BE AN IDIOT, YUSAKU... THE FESTIVALS HERE ARE PROBABLY BETTER, ANYWAY.

MIGHT BE NICE TO VISIT THE FOLKS, TOO.

THOSE WERE ALWAYS FUN...

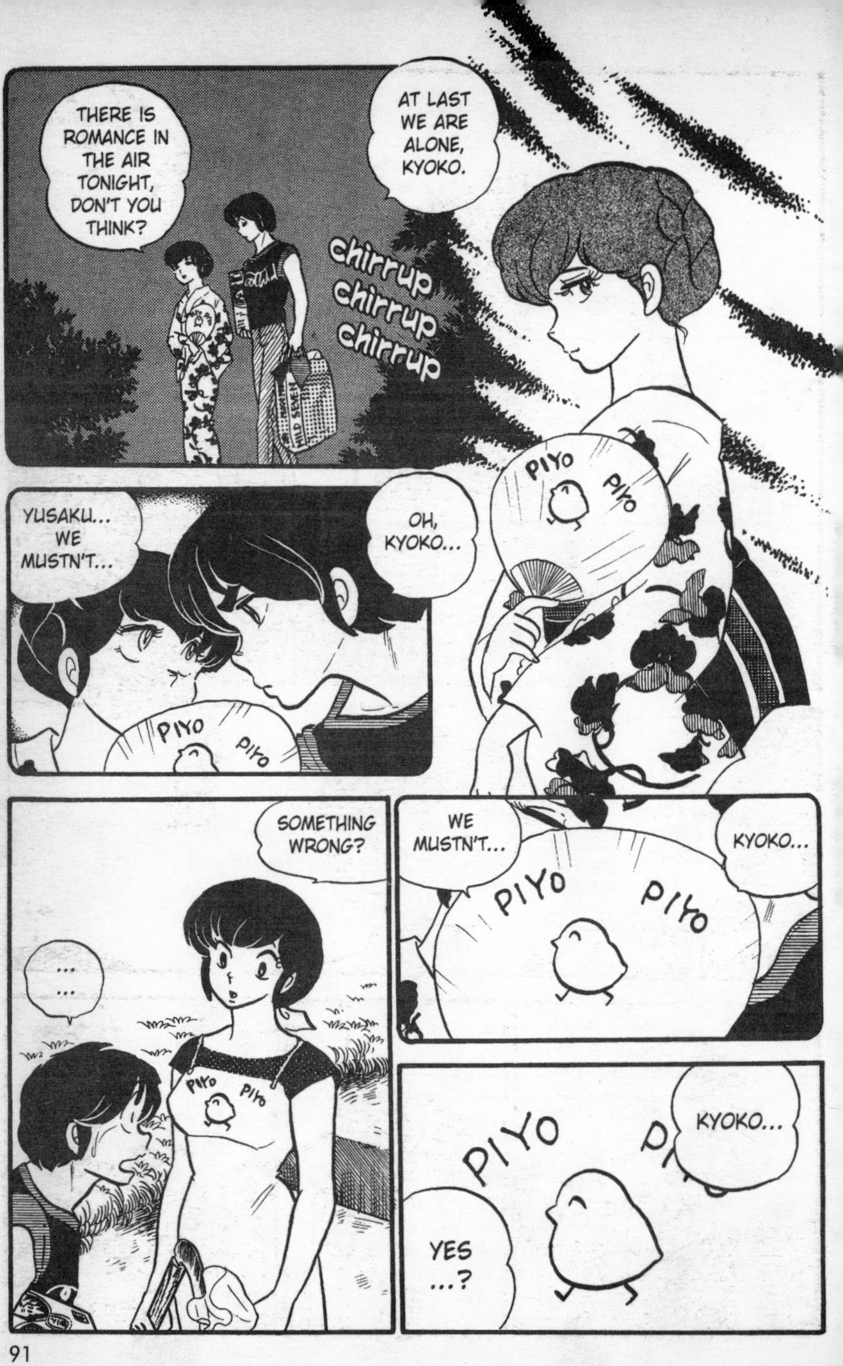
THERE IS ROMANCE IN THE AIR TONIGHT, DON'T YOU THINK?
AT LAST WE ARE ALONE, KYOKO.
chirrup chirrup chirrup
YUSAKU... WE MUSTN'T...
OH, KYOKO...
PIYO PIYO
PIYO PIYO
SOMETHING WRONG?
... ...
PIYO PIYO
WE MUSTN'T...
KYOKO...
PIYO PIYO
KYOKO...
YES ...?
PIYO

OH, I ALMOST FORGOT...

OH, WELL... IT'S THE FIRST TIME I'VE HAD ONE OF THOSE FANTASIES IN A WHILE.

YES, I CAN SEE THAT.

AH... ER... WELL, UM... I'M HOME!

THAT'S GREAT—THANKS!

I LEFT IT IN FRONT OF YOUR DOOR.

YOU GOT A BIG PARCEL FROM YOUR PARENTS.

WHOOSH

I NOTICED MR. YOTSUYA HANGING AROUND IT, THOUGH....

AH, MR. GODAI.

HEY!!

...
...

SNIK

BULL!

YOU HAVE COME AT A MOST FORTUITOUS MOMENT INDEED. ALTHOUGH I GREATLY WISHED TO OPEN THIS FINE PARCEL, I WAS VALIANTLY RESISTING THE URGE UNTIL YOU RETURNED.

HEY!!

AND SO...

STUFF STUFF

WHAT A MAGNIFICENT SIGHT... ALL THIS FINE FOOD...

I CAN DO THIS WITHOUT *YOUR* HELP, YOU MOOCHER.

...
...

HOW COLD-HEARTED!

LOOKS LIKE IT.

A SUMMER KIMONO, YES?

I'LL CALL YOU WHEN I GET SOME NEW SADNESS.

ALL THESE YEARS, WE'VE SHARED SO MANY THINGS... JOY AND SADNESS...

YOUR FREQUENT DONATIONS ARE MUCH APPRECIATED.

HERE'S A CAN OF PEACHES, SO BUG OFF, OKAY?

WELL, YOU'RE *NOT* GETTING THIS *ONE!!!*

AS YOU WILL OBSERVE, THIS ONE OF MINE IS QUITE OLD...

MAN, I'M POOPED.

I CAN WEAR IT AND —

THIS IS GREAT...

"Dear Yusaku — We figured you probably wouldn't make it back home this summer, so we sent this parcel.

This yukata was handmade for you by Grandma, so wear it at least once, okay?

Love, your Mom.

YES?

NOK NOK

GOOD QUESTION...

SAY... ARE YOU GOING TO WEAR A YUKATA TO THE FESTIVAL?

YEAH, MY GRANDMA MADE IT FOR ME.

OH, A YUKATA!

HEY, A FAN FOR THE LANTERN FESTIVAL DANCE!

UM... SOMEONE FROM THE LOCAL YOUTH ORGANIZATION DROPPED THESE BY.

I WILL BE GOING TO THE FESTIVAL, OF COURSE... AS A REPRESENTATIVE OF THIS APARTMENT BUILDING.

94

THANK YOU, GRANDMA!

YAHOO, YAHOO! ALL RIGHT!

...
...

TAP TAP TAP TAP **SLAM**

YEAH, MIGHT AS WELL! GREAT!

MIGHT AS WELL WEAR ONE, *HMM?*

OH, YUSAKU...

KYOKO...

PIYO

WHY, YUSAKU! I NEVER REALIZED WHAT A HANDSOME MAN YOU ARE!

AH, KYOKO... HOW RADIANT YOU LOOK THIS EVENING.

...
...

IT SEEMS NOTHING AT ALL HAS CHANGED IN THE PAST YEAR.

chirrup chirrup chirrup

A FESTIVAL? GREAT — I LOVE THEM!

YUUU-SAKU!

WHA-?!

WHY DOES THIS ALWAYS HAPPEN?

YUSAKU, YOU LOOK SO HANDSOME!

THANKS!

KYOKO, YOU LOOK POSITIVELY RADIANT!

KTAK

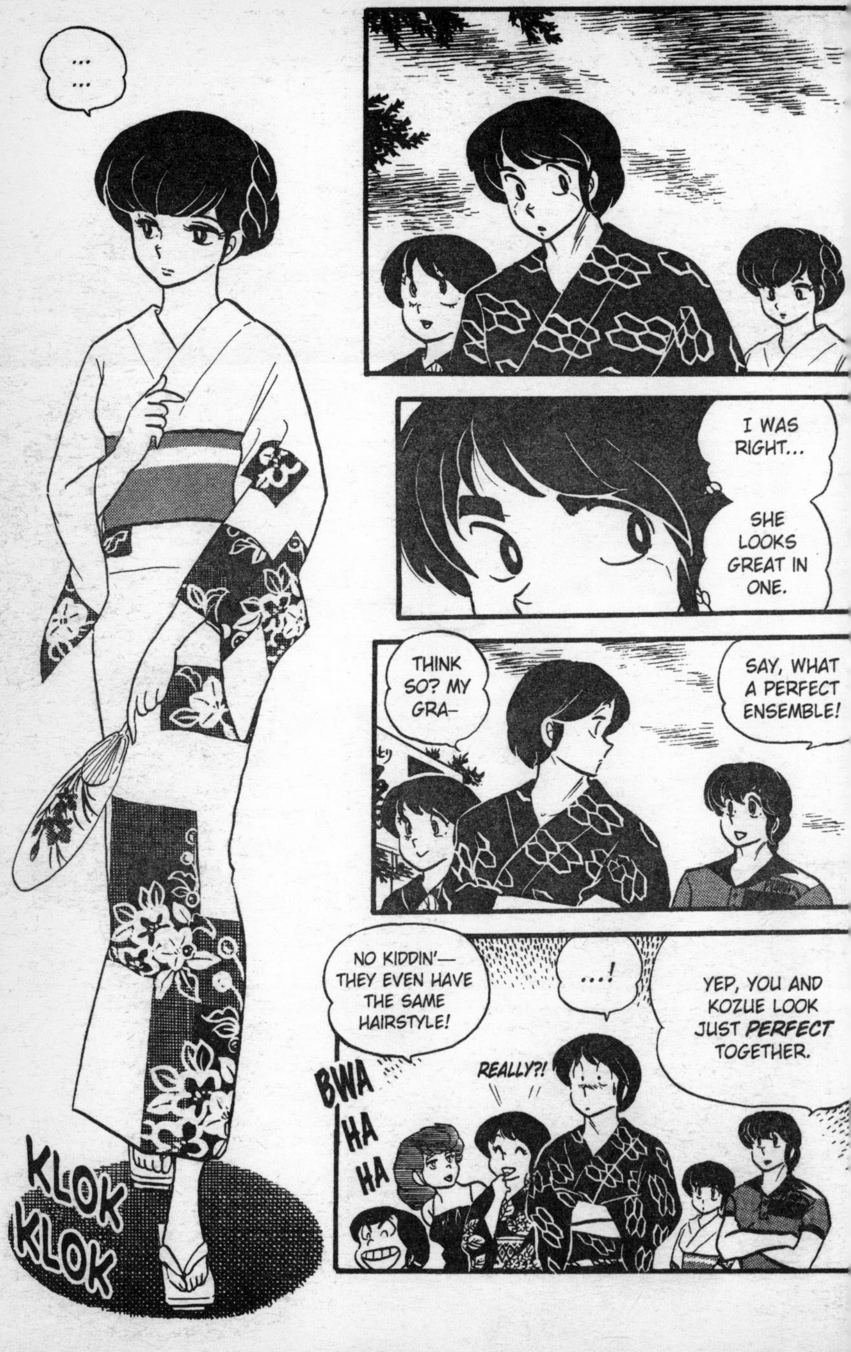
I WAS RIGHT...
SHE LOOKS GREAT IN ONE.
SAY, WHAT A PERFECT ENSEMBLE!
THINK SO? MY GRA-
YEP, YOU AND KOZUE LOOK JUST PERFECT TOGETHER.
...!
NO KIDDIN'— THEY EVEN HAVE THE SAME HAIRSTYLE!
REALLY?!
BWA HA HA
...
...
KLOK KLOK

WELL, I'M NOT VERY...

C'MON, SHUN — WIN ONE FOR ME!

HEY, YOU'RE PRETTY GOOD AT THAT.

ONE LITTLE FISHY, TWO LITTLE FISHIES...

SPLSH SPLSH

AW, C'MON — SIT DOWN RIGHT HERE!

ONE HUNDRED YEN PER CHANCE, SIR.

SHKK

MAY AS WELL TRY FOR THE BIGGEST ONE, THEN...

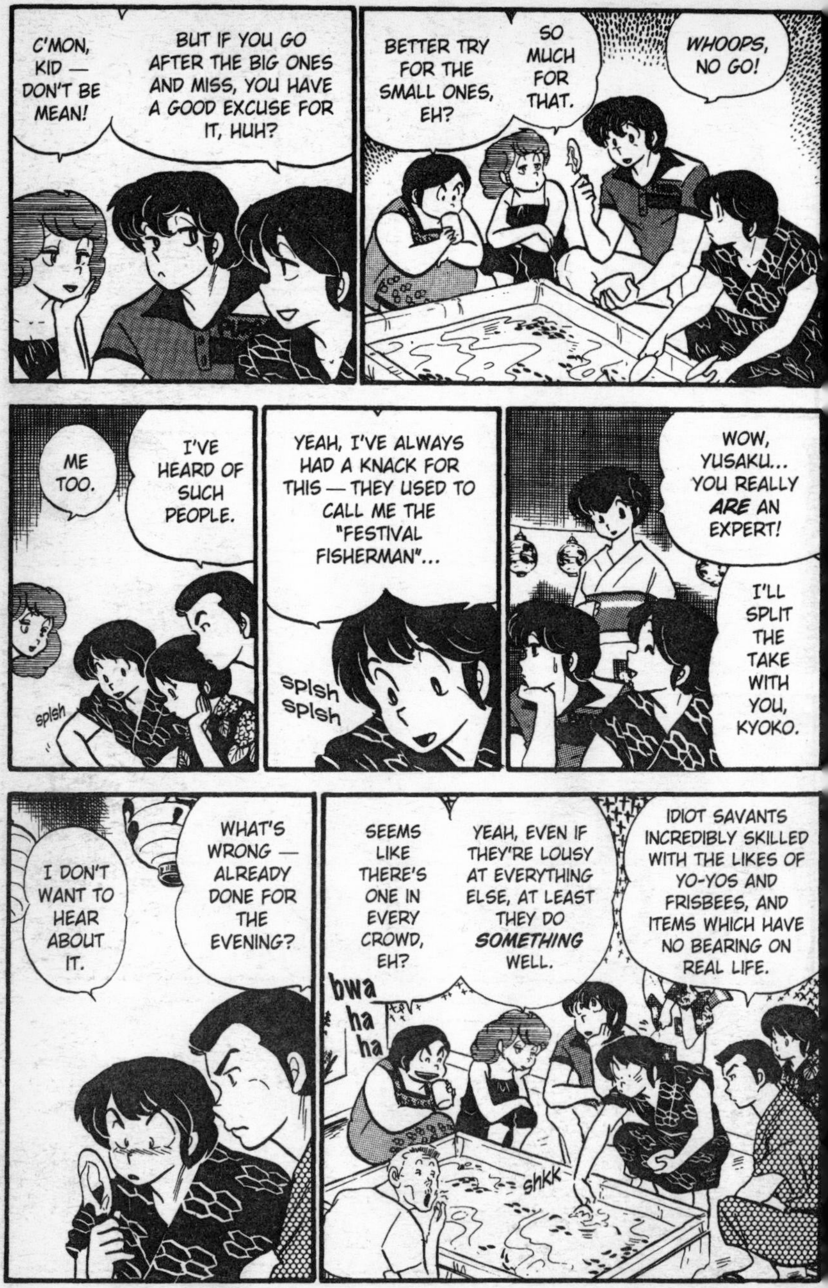
WHOOPS, NO GO!
SO MUCH FOR THAT.
BETTER TRY FOR THE SMALL ONES, EH?
BUT IF YOU GO AFTER THE BIG ONES AND MISS, YOU HAVE A GOOD EXCUSE FOR IT, HUH?
C'MON, KID — DON'T BE MEAN!
WOW, YUSAKU... YOU REALLY ARE AN EXPERT!
I'LL SPLIT THE TAKE WITH YOU, KYOKO.
YEAH, I'VE ALWAYS HAD A KNACK FOR THIS — THEY USED TO CALL ME THE "FESTIVAL FISHERMAN"...
splsh splsh
I'VE HEARD OF SUCH PEOPLE.
ME TOO.
splsh
IDIOT SAVANTS INCREDIBLY SKILLED WITH THE LIKES OF YO-YOS AND FRISBEES, AND ITEMS WHICH HAVE NO BEARING ON REAL LIFE.
YEAH, EVEN IF THEY'RE LOUSY AT EVERYTHING ELSE, AT LEAST THEY DO SOMETHING WELL.
SEEMS LIKE THERE'S ONE IN EVERY CROWD, EH?
bwa ha ha
shkk
WHAT'S WRONG — ALREADY DONE FOR THE EVENING?
I DON'T WANT TO HEAR ABOUT IT.

YEAH, RIGHT.

TOO BAD "FESTIVAL FISHING" AIN'T A PRO SPORT, EH, KID?

HERE YOU GO.

WOW, THANK YOU!

LET'S ALL GO.

I THINK I'M GOING TO GO WATCH THE LANTERN DANCE.

TOOO-KYO ONNN-DO

Oooh!

aaah!

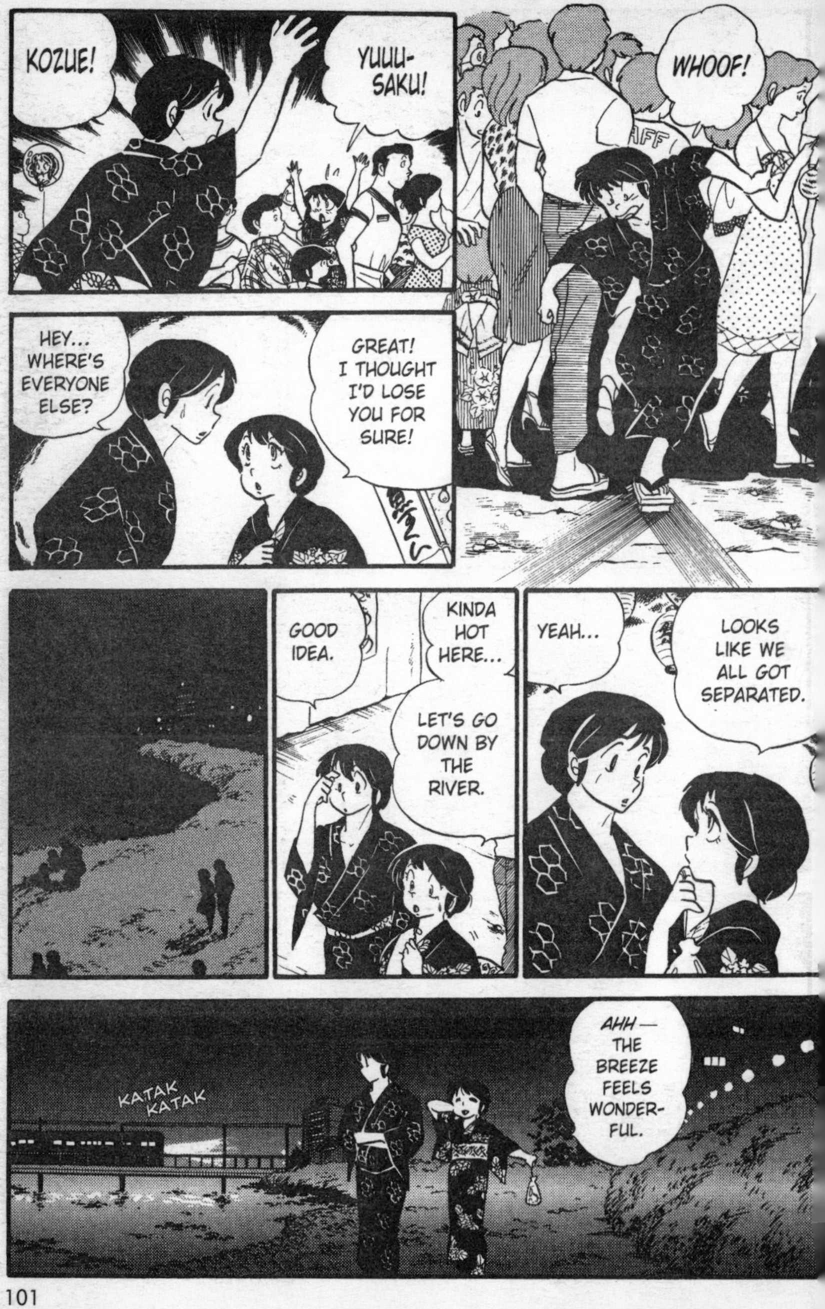
WHOOF!
YUUU-SAKU!
KOZUE!
GREAT! I THOUGHT I'D LOSE YOU FOR SURE!
HEY... WHERE'S EVERYONE ELSE?
LOOKS LIKE WE ALL GOT SEPARATED.
YEAH...
KINDA HOT HERE...
LET'S GO DOWN BY THE RIVER.
GOOD IDEA.
AHH— THE BREEZE FEELS WONDER-FUL.
KATAK KATAK

WHSSHH

HMM...

bink
bink

SHE'S PRETTY CUTE, WHEN I REALLY LOOK AT HER.

HOLD IT, PAL.

NO POINT STARTING SOMETHING.

...NOBODY AROUND BUT OTHER COUPLES...

ON THE OTHER HAND...

NO, NO, NOT AT ALL. IT'S A LITTLE "HOT AND HEAVY" AROUND HERE FOR ME, ANYWAY.

UMM... WOULD YOU MIND TERRIBLY IF WE WENT SOMEWHERE ELSE?

GOOD QUESTION.

I WONDER WHERE THE OTHERS ENDED UP...

LOOKS QUIETER OVER THAT WAY...

THAT SWINE! HE'S LURING HER OFF INTO THE DARKNESS!

THERE'S NOBODY AROUND OVER THERE...

JUST OVER THIS WAY.

WHERE ARE WE GOING?

...
...

MAYBE *TOO* QUIET.

NICE OVER HERE... QUIET, LOTS OF TREES...

NO...

YES...

HE'S JUST NOT THAT KIND OF GUY.

I MEAN, SHUN IS A GROWN-UP... UNLIKE YUSAKU...

ON THE OTHER HAND... SHE SURE DIDN'T SEEM TO *MIND* COMING HERE WITH ME... SO MAYBE...

...SHE'LL THINK I DELIBERATELY LURED HER HERE FOR THAT.

IF I MAKE A PASS AT HER *NOW*...

THOOM DOOM BATHOOM

...
...

...
...

DAMN... WHAT TO DO?

AND IF I SUDDENLY SAID, "LET'S GO BACK TO THE FESTIVAL...."

IT WOULD LOOK LIKE I DIDN'T TRUST HIM.

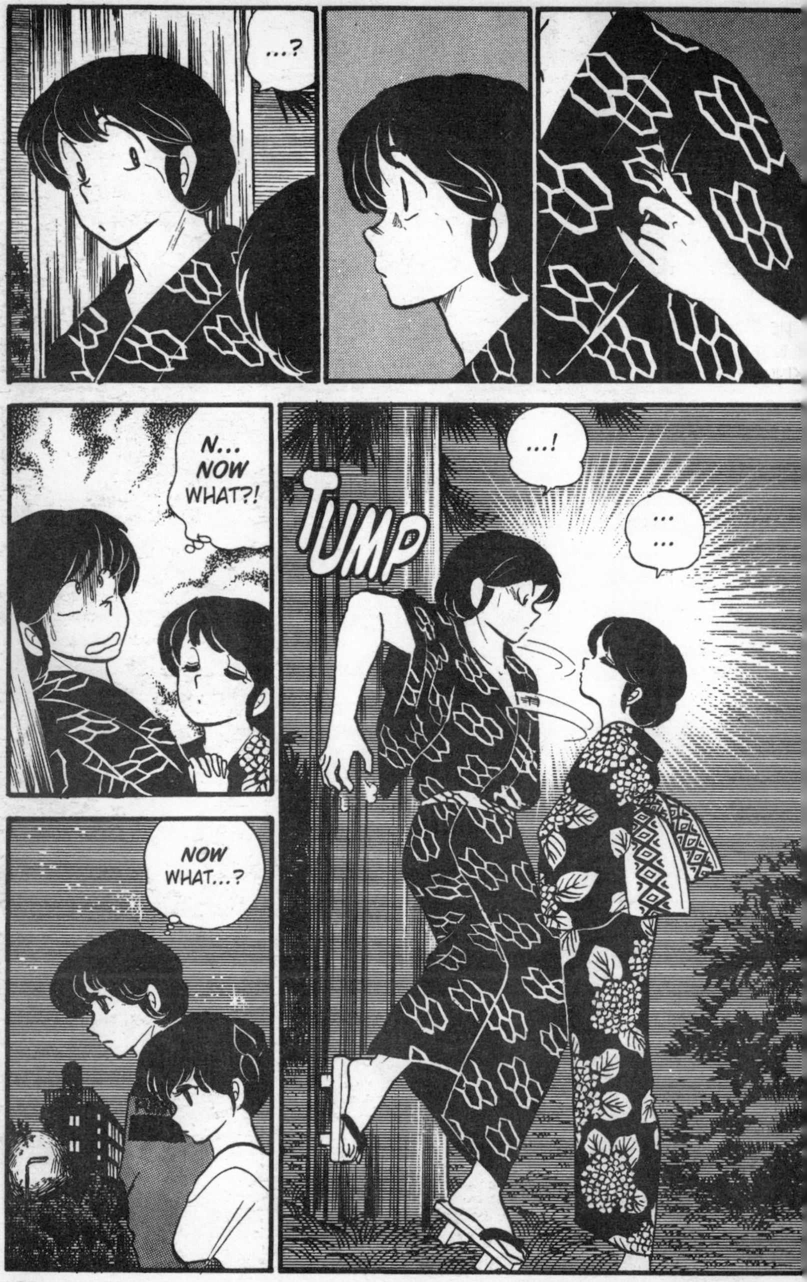
...?
N... NOW WHAT?!
NOW WHAT...?
TUMP
...!
... ...

KYOKO...

AND SHE REALLY MEANS SOMETHING TO ME!

DAMN IT ALL, *NOTHING'S* EVER GOING TO HAPPEN IF I JUST SUFFER IN SILENCE!

DO YOU LIKE ME?

IF NOT, JUST TELL ME, OKAY?

B...

BUT...

...

...

WELL? DO YOU?

TELL ME AND I'LL STOP RIGHT HERE.

I... I... I JUST...

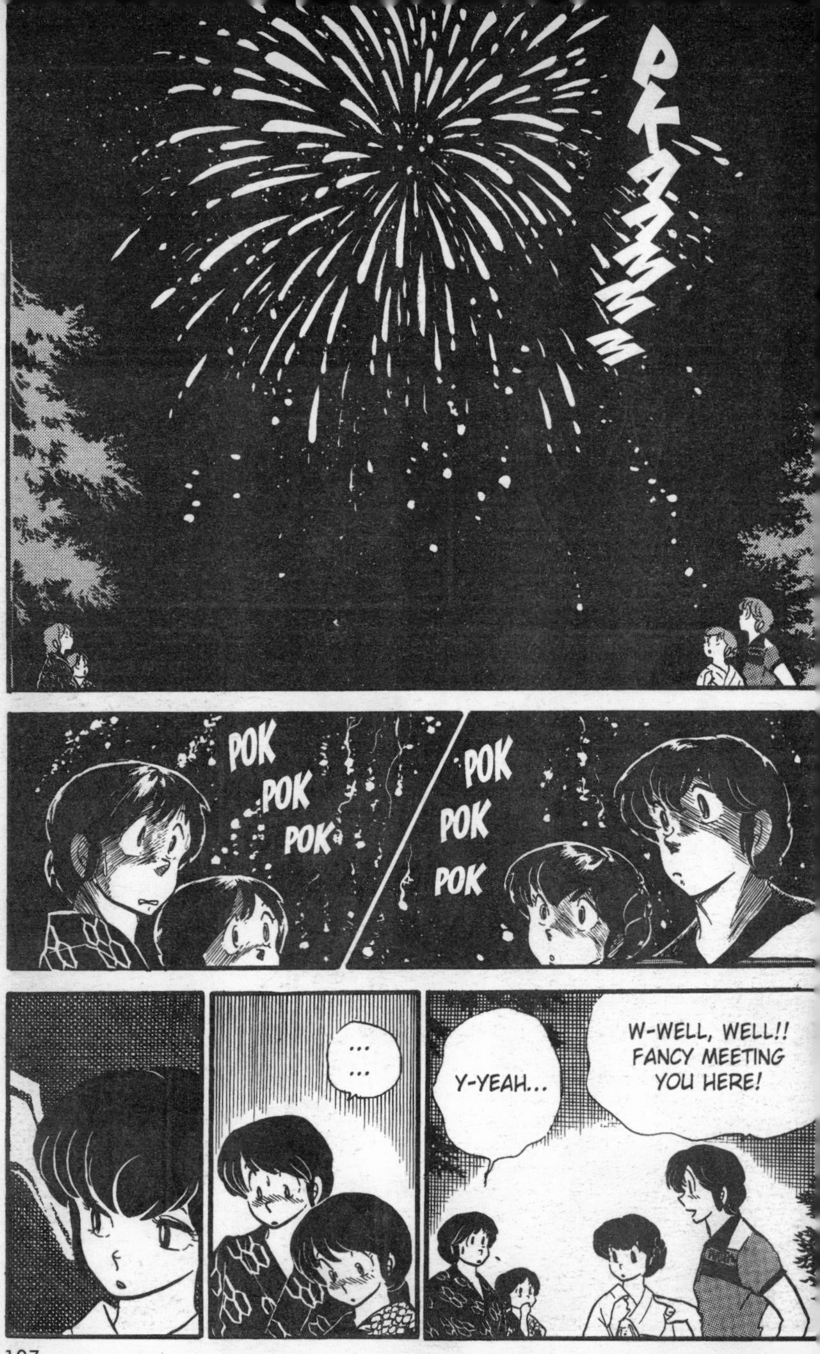
PKAAMMM
POK
POK
POK
POK
POK
POK
...
...
Y-YEAH...
W-WELL, WELL!! FANCY MEETING YOU HERE!

OKAY...

I PARKED MY CAR DOWN BY THE STATION, SO I'LL SAY GOODBYE HERE.

THE LANTERN DANCE WILL BE HELD ONCE MORE TOMORROW EVENING, STARTING FROM 7 P.M...

THANK YOU FOR ATTENDING OUR FESTIVAL, AND PLEASE COME AGAIN.

PLEASE DON'T WORRY ABOUT IT.

I'M SORRY ABOUT THAT —

UM...

REALLY?! THAT'S GREAT! THANKS, MR. MITAKA!

IF YOU WANT, I CAN GIVE YOU A RIDE, KOZUE.

YEAH...

WELL... SEE YOU, YUSAKU.

WHAT'S *HE* BLUSHING FOR?

I'M SURE KOZUE WOULD HAVE PREFERRED FOR *YOU* TO SEE HER HOME, YUSAKU.

YEAH, I DIDN'T SEE YOU AROUND ANYWHERE.

HEY, MR. YOTSUYA! WHAT DID YOU DO AFTER WE GOT SPLIT UP?

JUST *WHAT* WERE THEY DOING, ALL ALONE IN THAT PLACE...?

I WAS INDULGING IN A BIT OF VOYEURISM...

URK!

EEP!

LEAN CLOSE AND I WILL WHISPER...

NO KIDDIN'... ANY HOT COUPLES?

LOOK, YOU — VOYEURISM IS A *CRIME!*

I WAS TRAGICALLY DISAPPOINTED IN YOUR BEHAVIOR, YOUNG GODAI.

YUSAKU AND KOZUE!

DAMN IT, YOTSUYA!

WHADDA **YOU** KNOW, PERVERT?!

THE **REAL** CRIME IS TO RESIST A GIRL'S ADVANCES WHEN SHE THROWS HERSELF AT YOU IN THAT MANNER.

PRETTY SAD, KIDDO...

WELL, WELL... SO HE FROZE UP, EH?

I'D BETTER GO BUY A FISHBOWL TOMORROW.

CHINGG

spish

SO...

...NOTHING HAPPENED.

PART SIX
MEMORIES OF YOU

NNNNGH. WHAT A BOR-RING SUMMER THIS'S BEEN!

WELLLLLL... NOT FOR ME IT HASN'T!

YOU'RE KIDDING! FINALLY!

MY BOYFRIEND AND I... FINALLY WENT ALL THE WAY!

WELL, FIRST WE WENT TO THE BEACH...

SO HOW WAS HE?

...SO, LIKE Y'KNOW, HE...

...I WAS KINDA NERVOUS, BUT...

...AND LIKE THAT.

...THEN WE...

...AND THEN...

YUSAKU GODAI, ISN'T IT?

YEAH, YOU'VE GOT A BOYFRIEND, RIGHT?

SO HOW ABOUT YOU, KOZUE?

WOW...

YOU THINK?

AH, KOZUE. YOU'RE STILL SUCH A KID.

WELL, WE HAVEN'T REALLY... Y'KNOW.

THAT'S PRETTY WEIRD.

AND YOU'RE TELLING US YOU HAVEN'T DONE *ANYTHING*?

YOU GUYS HAVE BEEN DATING FOR ABOUT A YEAR, RIGHT?

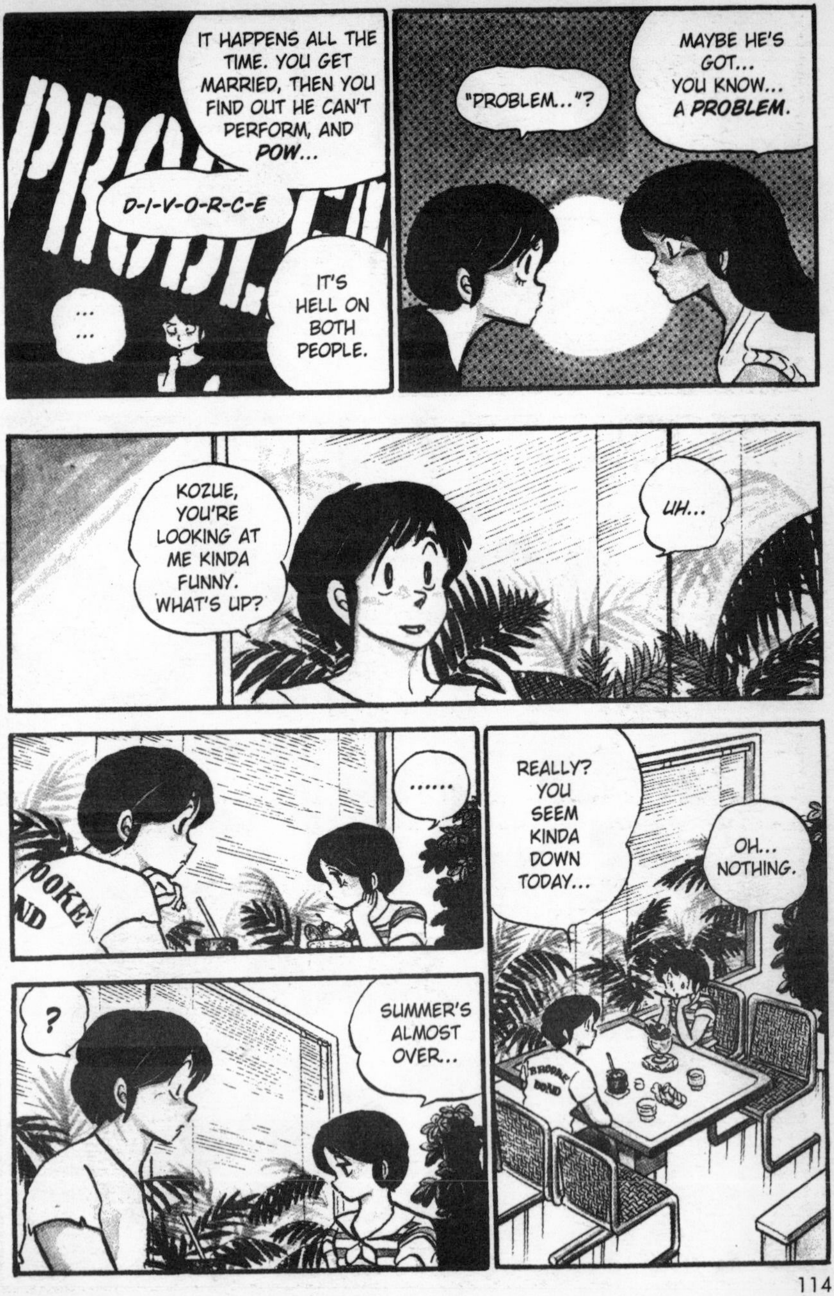
IT HAPPENS ALL THE TIME. YOU GET MARRIED, THEN YOU FIND OUT HE CAN'T PERFORM, AND POW...
D-I-V-O-R-C-E
IT'S HELL ON BOTH PEOPLE.
... ...
MAYBE HE'S GOT... YOU KNOW... A PROBLEM.
"PROBLEM..."?
KOZUE, YOU'RE LOOKING AT ME KINDA FUNNY. WHAT'S UP?
UH...
......
REALLY? YOU SEEM KINDA DOWN TODAY...
OH... NOTHING.
?
SUMMER'S ALMOST OVER...

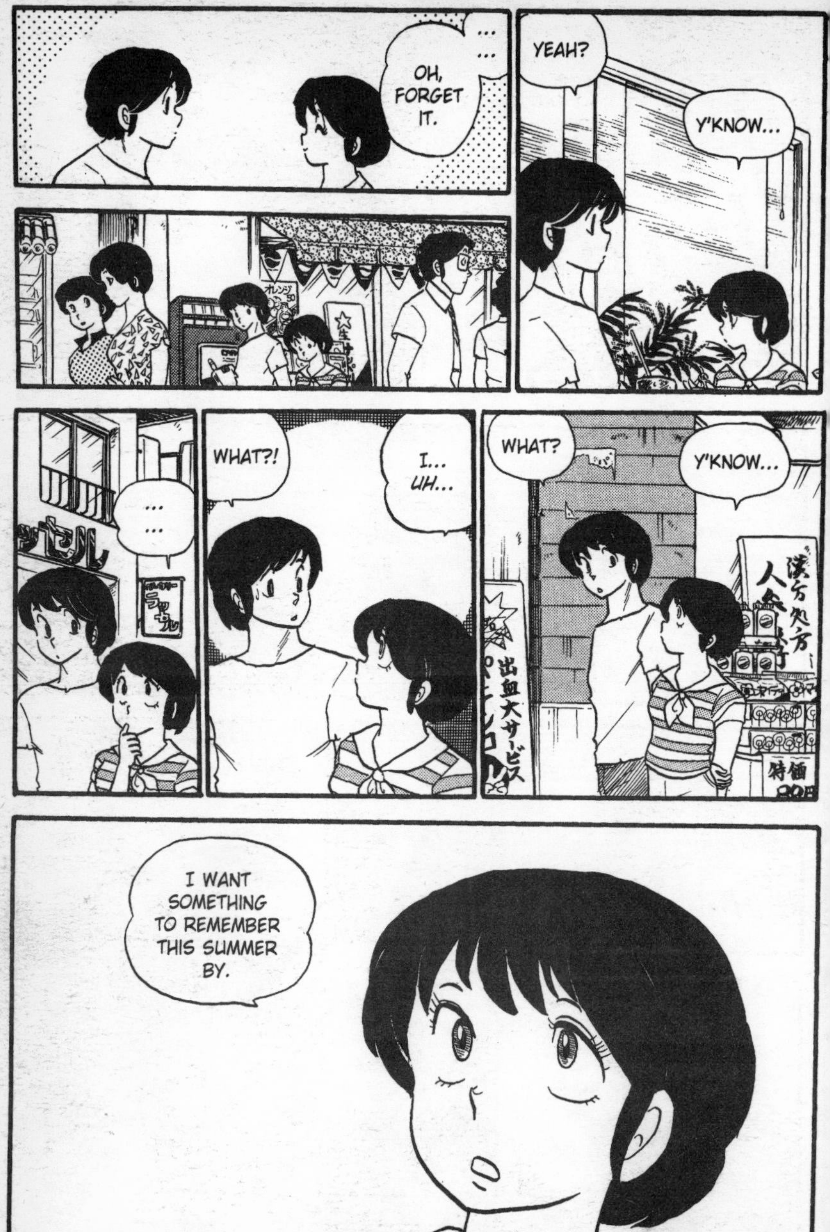
Y'KNOW...
YEAH?
... ...
OH, FORGET IT.
Y'KNOW...
WHAT?
I... UH...
WHAT?!
... ...
I WANT SOMETHING TO REMEMBER THIS SUMMER BY.
オレンジ 50
出血大サービス
特価

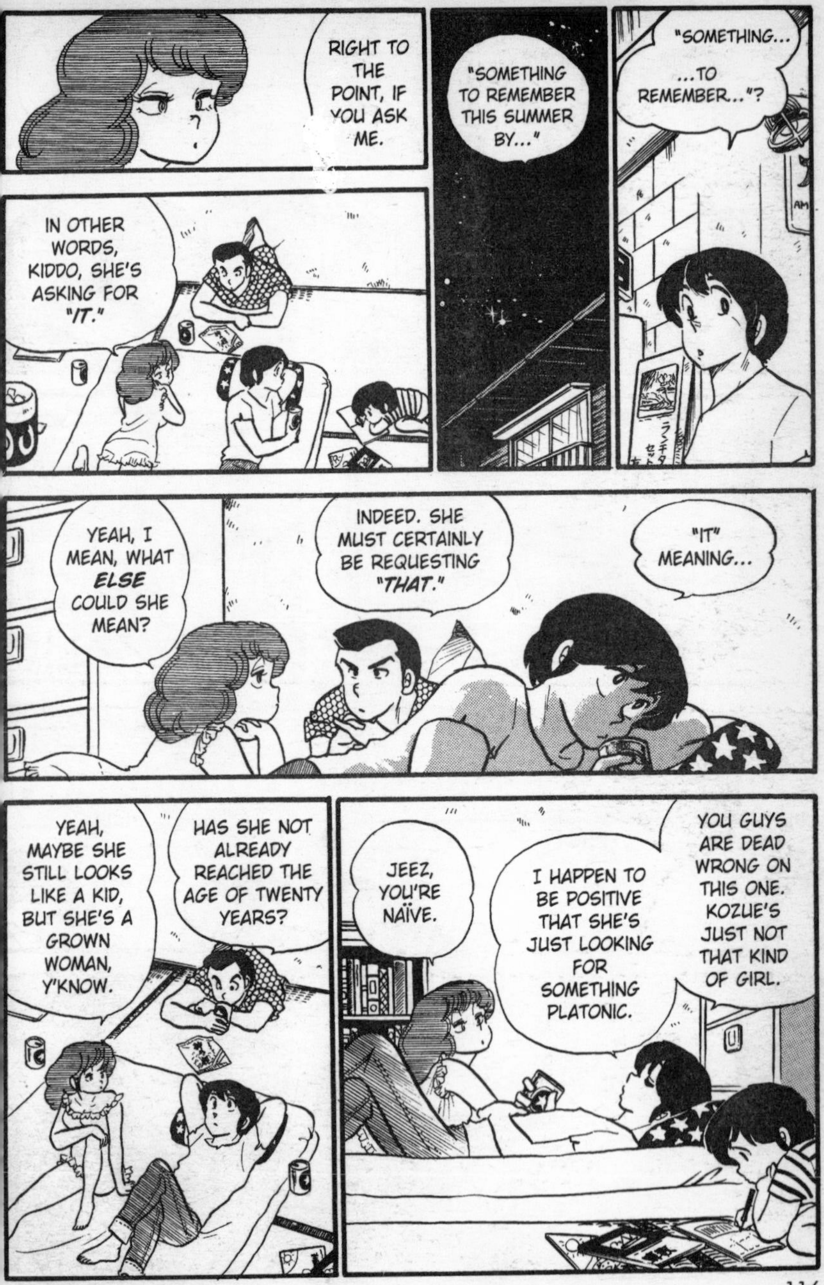

RIGHT TO THE POINT, IF YOU ASK ME.
"SOMETHING TO REMEMBER THIS SUMMER BY..."
"SOMETHING...
...TO REMEMBER..."?
IN OTHER WORDS, KIDDO, SHE'S ASKING FOR "IT."
YEAH, I MEAN, WHAT ELSE COULD SHE MEAN?
INDEED. SHE MUST CERTAINLY BE REQUESTING "THAT."
"IT" MEANING...
YEAH, MAYBE SHE STILL LOOKS LIKE A KID, BUT SHE'S A GROWN WOMAN, Y'KNOW.
HAS SHE NOT ALREADY REACHED THE AGE OF TWENTY YEARS?
JEEZ, YOU'RE NAÏVE.
I HAPPEN TO BE POSITIVE THAT SHE'S JUST LOOKING FOR SOMETHING PLATONIC.
YOU GUYS ARE DEAD WRONG ON THIS ONE. KOZUE'S JUST NOT THAT KIND OF GIRL.

MAYBE SHE REALLY *DOES* WANT TO...

STILL... MAYBE THEY'RE RIGHT.

WELL, WELL!

IT'S JUST NOT THAT KIND OF RELATIONSHIP.

CUT IT OUT, YOU GUYS.

DID I? OKAY, THEN.

DON'T FORGET, YOU *PROMISED!*

HEY, YOU GONNA HELP ME WITH MY HOMEWORK OR WHAT?!

DOES "SOMETHING" REALLY MEAN "*DOING IT...*"?

DON'T FORGET TO REDO IT LATER IN YOUR OWN HANDWRITING.

'KAY.

OKAY.

HOW DID THE TUTORING GO?

Exercise 3: Verbs: *Words that describe actions*

Fill in the blank in each sentence with a verb
(examples: run, play, etc.)

Yoshiko: "Masao, wouldn't you like to _do it_?"

Masao: "Can we _do it_ there?" Masao points to a grassy meadow.

Yoshiko: "No. Let's _do it_ at my place."

Masao: "Will your parents mind if we _do it_ at your place?"

Yoshiko: "No, I _do it_ there with all my friends."

118

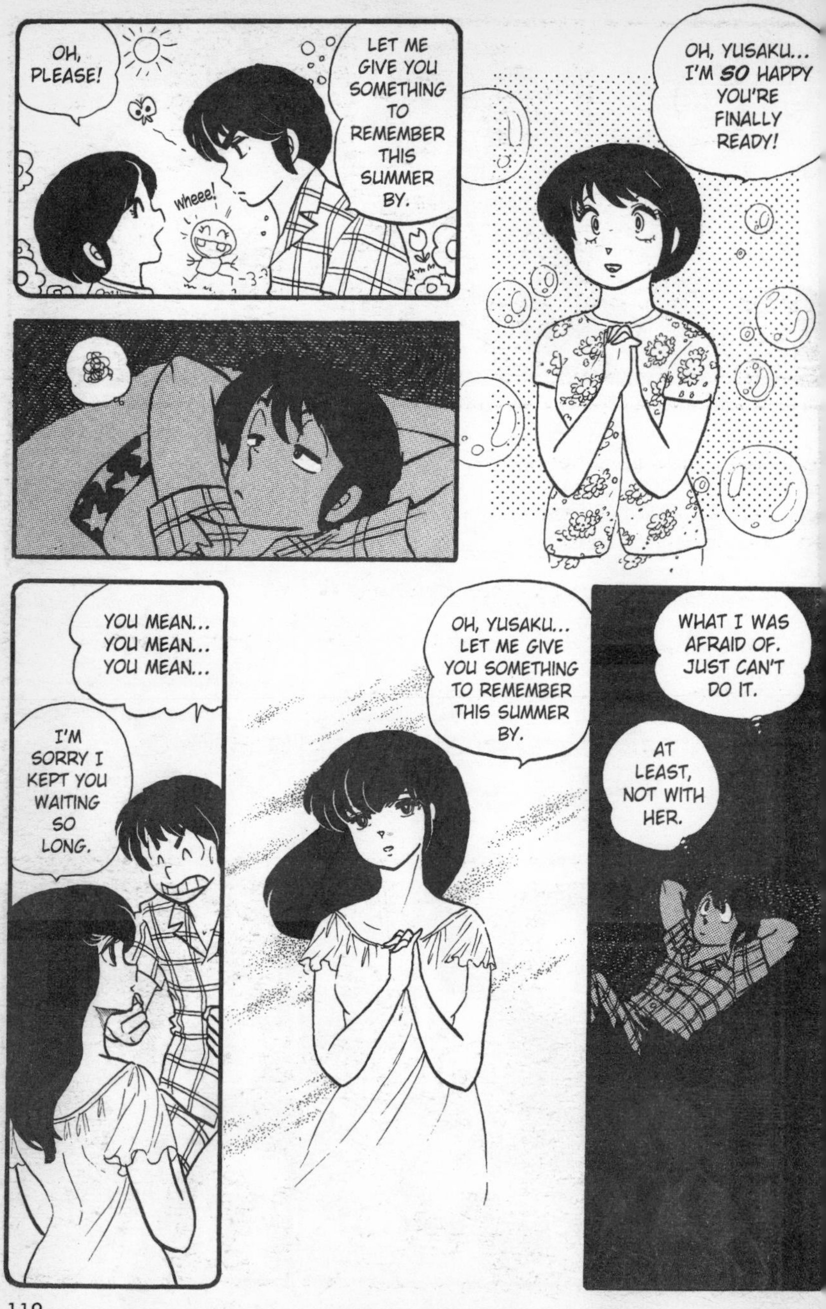

OH, PLEASE!
wheee!
LET ME GIVE YOU SOMETHING TO REMEMBER THIS SUMMER BY.
OH, YUSAKU... I'M SO HAPPY YOU'RE FINALLY READY!
YOU MEAN... YOU MEAN... YOU MEAN...
I'M SORRY I KEPT YOU WAITING SO LONG.
OH, YUSAKU... LET ME GIVE YOU SOMETHING TO REMEMBER THIS SUMMER BY.
WHAT I WAS AFRAID OF. JUST CAN'T DO IT.
AT LEAST, NOT WITH HER.

I'M SO GLAD I SAVED MYSELF FOR YOU!

OH, YUSAKU!

...DONE IT!

GASP

KYOKO...

...IS A WIDOW!

THAT MEANS SHE WAS MARRIED...

AND THAT MEANS SHE'S...

HAVE FUN!

I'M GOIN' OVER TO SAKA-MOTO'S PLACE.

I JUST DON'T KNOW WHERE TO START...

—AND SO...?

Kyoko Baby, you're so big now!

WAIT A SEC... I GOTTA GET MY HEAD STRAIGHT ON THIS.

PROBABLY. BUT DON'T GO TOO FAST.

WELL, ANYWAY, YEAH — I GUESS KOZUE WANTS TO. SEEMS LIKE IT, ANYWAY.

YOU GUYS SURE GET RIGHT TO THE POINT, DON'T YOU?

YOU STILL HAVEN'T, *HUH*?

YOU MEAN ABOUT GETTIN' IT ON?

NO, NO, THAT'S NOT WHAT I MEAN.

I MEAN...

ROMANCE, THAT'S THE KEY — A NICE ROMANTIC SETTING, TO START WITH.

YEAH, IF YOU JUST, Y'KNOW, GO FOR IT, SHE'LL PROBABLY FREAK.

THAT'LL BE *NEVER!*

YOU PLANNIN' ON WAITIN' AROUND UNTIL YOUR MANAGER JUMPS ON YOU OR SOMETHING?

YOU'RE ALREADY 21.

AHH... I DON'T EVEN KNOW *WHAT* I MEAN!

URK!

URK!

YEAH, WHY NOT? UNLESS YOU GOT SOME KINDA *PROBLEM....*

HEY, IF KOZUE'S BEGGIN' FOR IT, WHY NOT?

I JUST HAVEN'T BROUGHT HIM HOME FOR A WHILE, THAT'S ALL.

KONK

YEAH, MAYBE SIS GOT DUMPED — OW!

WE HAVEN'T SEEN YUSAKU AROUND FOR QUITE A WHILE, HAVE WE, DEAR?

HE SURE IS.

WELL, I HOPE HE'S BEING A GENTLEMAN.

RIGHT! YOU'RE NOT A CHILD ANYMORE, HONEY — IT'S ABOUT TIME YOU STARTED THINKING ABOUT HAVING A SERIOUS RELATIONSHIP.

BUT THAT'S WONDERFUL, DEAR— YOU CAN TRUST HIM NOT TO TAKE ADVANTAGE, THEN.

I DON'T THINK HE'S GOT THE NERVE TO BE ANYTHING BUT. HE'S SO NAÏVE...

I DUNNO... A CHILL JUST WENT DOWN MY SPINE!

WHAT'S UP?

BLAMMO

DAD'S A GOOD SHOT, TOO!

AND IF HE EVER DOES *ANYTHING* TO MAKE MY LITTLE GIRL UNHAPPY, JUST LET ME KNOW AND I'LL SHOOT HIM DEAD FOR YOU! HEH HEH!

NOW, FATHER, YOU CAN'T BE SERIOUS!

"IF YOU DON'T GET IN SOME PRACTICE BEFOREHAND, SHE'LL THINK YOU'RE A TOTAL GEEK."

"YOUR MANAGER'S AN OLDER WOMAN SHE'S GOT EXPERIENCE."

"YOU PLANNIN' ON WAITIN' AROUND UNTIL YOUR MANAGER JUMPS ON YOU OR SOMETHING?"

KATAK KATAK

YEAH... HOW LONG *SHOULD* I WAIT?

...

...

MAYBE, BUT...

"C'MON, YUSAKU — EVEN IF YOU SLEEP WITH KOZUE, THAT DOESN'T MEAN YOU GOTTA MARRY HER OR..."

"I LOVE YOU."

YES, MY DEAR, I NEED SOME PRAC— ER, I MEAN—

OH, YUSAKU, YOU'VE MADE ME SO HAPPY!

SO YOU'VE DONE IT AT LAST!

WHAM

OH, YUSAKU... I'M *SO* HAPPY YOU'RE FINALLY READY!

SEE YOU LATER!

HURRY HOME, SWEETIE!

BYE-BYE, DA-DA!

I... BUT... NO, WAIT!

HALLELUJAH!

NOW THAT YOU'VE "DONE IT," OF COURSE YOU'LL MAKE AN HONEST WOMAN OF MY DAUGHTER. *HEH HEH.*

LET'S CELEBRATE!

I WONDER HOW *SHE* IS DOING...?

NOTHING'S REALLY WRONG WITH MY LIFE, AND YET...

I FEEL SO EMPTY INSIDE...

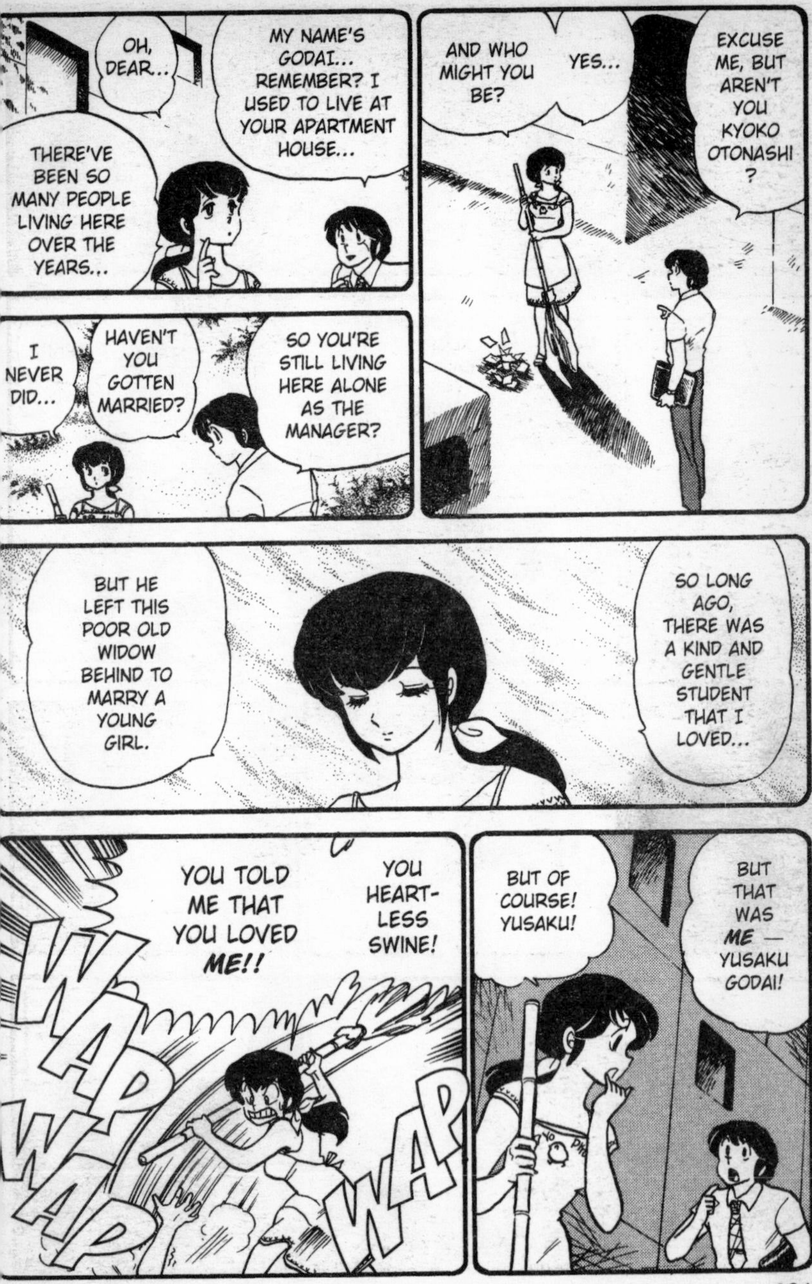
EXCUSE ME, BUT AREN'T YOU KYOKO OTONASHI ?
YES...
AND WHO MIGHT YOU BE?
MY NAME'S GODAI... REMEMBER? I USED TO LIVE AT YOUR APARTMENT HOUSE...
OH, DEAR...
THERE'VE BEEN SO MANY PEOPLE LIVING HERE OVER THE YEARS...
SO YOU'RE STILL LIVING HERE ALONE AS THE MANAGER?
HAVEN'T YOU GOTTEN MARRIED?
I NEVER DID...
SO LONG AGO, THERE WAS A KIND AND GENTLE STUDENT THAT I LOVED...
BUT HE LEFT THIS POOR OLD WIDOW BEHIND TO MARRY A YOUNG GIRL.
BUT THAT WAS *ME* — YUSAKU GODAI!
BUT OF COURSE! YUSAKU!
YOU HEARTLESS SWINE!
YOU TOLD ME THAT YOU LOVED *ME!!*
WAP
WAP
WAP
WAP

IT COULD RUIN MY WHOLE LIFE!

I JUST CAN'T!

IT'S ME.

HELLO, KOZUE?

ulp!

KOZUE CALLED WHILE YOU WERE OUT.

SORRY I'M BACK SO LATE.

HI YUSAKU.

YEAH... COME OVER TO MY HOUSE ABOUT LUNCHTIME, 'KAY?

TOMOR-ROW?

SO WHAT'S UP?

AH, THERE YOU ARE!

THE NEXT DAY...

HELLO ...?

127

TAKE OFF YOUR SHIRT.

....!

"SOMETHING TO REMEMBER.."

EVERYBODY'S GONE OUT.

WHERE ARE YOUR FOLKS?

HUH?

PUT ON THE SHIRT IN THAT BAG, OKAY?

I'LL GO OUT, THEN.

I CAN'T, I COULDN'T...

LOOK, KOZUE!

WELL, MAYBE A LITTLE KISS...

OH, SORRY.

BUT...

GREAT! LET'S GO...

...AND DO SOMETHING TO REMEMBER!

?

SO **THIS** IS YOUR BOYFRIEND!

...

...

YOU LOOK SO CUTE TOGETHER!

BLAB BLAB

THIS IS ALL SHE MEANS BY "SOMETHING TO REMEMBER..."?

WHAT THE HECK...?

BLAB BLAB

BLAB BLAB BLAB

BUT I GOTTA ASK — WHY?

...

...

AW, DON'T WORRY ABOUT IT.

SORRY I DRAGGED YOU ALONG TODAY.

I KINDA WANTED TO SHOW YOU OFF TO MY FRIENDS, I GUESS.

129

...I'D FALL IN LOVE WITH YOU, KOZUE.

IF THERE WASN'T ANY KYOKO...

ANYWAY, THAT'S ALL.

HA, HA!

HEE, HEE!

KONK

REPENT

MAYBE JUST ONE KISS...

...MY DEAR KOZUE.

PART SEVEN
THE INCIDENT

SURE!

COULD I SPEAK WITH YOU FOR A MOMENT, KYOKO?

OKAY, EVERYONE, THAT'S ALL FOR TODAY.

ABSOLUTELY POSITIVE. SO IS THAT A YES?

YES.

OKAY...

IT'D BE NICE IF YOU COULD GIVE ME AN ANSWER SOON...

...BUT ARE YOU SURE I'M THE RIGHT PERSON FOR YOU?

I'M SORRY... I DON'T KNOW WHY I DIDN'T SAY YES RIGHT AWAY.

I'D PRETTY MUCH GIVEN UP, YOU KNOW...

THAT'S GREAT!

...SINCE YOU'D MADE ME WAIT FOR SO LONG.

DSB

SO, DID YOU KNOW ABOUT THIS?

THERE'S NO DOUBT ABOUT WHAT *THAT* MEANS!

DID YOU HEAR *THAT*?!

"ME? I WAS MY USUAL CLUELESS SELF..."

"I ONLY HEARD ABOUT THIS MUCH, MUCH LATER, BUT THEY SAID THAT AT THE TIME, MRS. ICHINOSE SEEMED PRETTY DEPRESSED BY THE SITUATION."

I CAN'T BELIEVE THEY'VE GOTTEN SO SERIOUS.

IT'S NEWS TO ME.

JUST WHEN YOU THINK YOU KNOW A PERSON...

I THOUGHT I WAS PRETTY CLOSE TO KYOKO, THOUGHT SHE'D TELL ME EVERYTHING.

HMM?

STUDIO WITH BATH, ¥40,000...

NOT *TOO* BAD...

HEY, KYOKO! HI!

YUSAKU...?

WELL...

A CHEAP STUDIO WITH BATH.

UM...

WHAT ARE YOU LOOKING FOR?

YEAH, GOTTA HAVE IT.

YOU'RE LOOKING FOR ONE WITH A PRIVATE BATH, ARE YOU?

AHA! ONLY 15 MINUTES WALK FROM THE STATION.

¥50,000!! OUCH!

......

ME?!

EH?

ARE... ARE YOU GOING TO MOVE OUT?

...
...

PHEW!

DON'T SCARE ME LIKE THAT, YUSAKU!

I'M JUST HELPING OUT A PAL.

MOVE OUT?! YOU GOTTA BE *KIDDING!*

IT'S KINDA STRANGE IF YOU THINK ABOUT IT...

Y-YEAH... TRUE.

WELL...

...THE TENANTS AT IKKOKU DON'T REALLY CHANGE, DO THEY?

WHY'S THAT?

I SEE...

GUESS THAT'S WHY I WAS SO SURPRISED JUST NOW.

......

I GUESS THAT SOMEDAY, EVERYONE WILL HAVE MOVED OUT AND BE SCATTERED TO THE WINDS.

BUT IT'S JUST KIND OF HARD TO BELIEVE THAT DAY WILL EVER COME.

ACTUALLY, BEFORE I FINALLY PASSED MY ENTRANCE EXAMS, I THOUGHT ABOUT MOVING OUT A LOT, BUT NOW...

WELL, SHE SEEMS GENUINELY PLEASED, ANYWAY.

I WONDER WHAT SHE MEANS BY THAT.

I'M REALLY GLAD TO HEAR THAT, YUSAKU.

NOW I'D NEVER CONSIDER LEAVING.

IT FEELS LIKE HOME TO ME.

I GUESS EVEN A GUY LIKE ME IS BETTER THAN NOTHING.

136

heh heh

ONCE IN A WHILE SHE'LL SAY SOME-THING LIKE THAT...

SHE'S A WICKED WOMAN.

...SOME-THING TO MAKE ME THINK SHE MIGHT REALLY CARE...

...AND SO SHE KEEPS ME HANGING ONTO MY DREAMS.

SO YOUNG YUSAKU IS IN A GOOD MOOD, IS HE?

HAH... HOW MUCH YOU WANNA BET OUR CUTE LI'L MANAGER IS INVOLVED?

DON'T EVEN BOTHER, AKEMI.

NOTHING YOU SAY COULD SPOIL MY GOOD MOOD.

YOU'RE GIVIN' ME THE CREEPS WITH THAT GRIN ON YOUR FACE.

JEEZ, YUSAKU, WHAT HAPPENED TO *YOU* TODAY?

I HEARD THAT—

OH, YEAH, I HEARD ABOUT IT, ALL RIGHT.

AH, YES... SPEAKING OF OUR HONORABLE MANAGER.. HAVE YOU HEARD THE TRAGIC TALE FROM MRS. ICHINOSE?

C'MON YOU TWO – SPILL!

SOMETHING'S UP WITH KYOKO, ISN'T IT?

YEAH, YOU'LL JUST GET ALL BENT OUTTA SHAPE.

YOU MUST NOT LISTEN TO THIS.

ABOUT WHAT? WHAT?!

......

"COACH MITAKA."

YEAH, *RIGHT.* C'MON, HOW BAD CAN IT BE?

WE WERE TAKING EXTRAORDINARY MEASURES TO PROTECT YOU FROM THIS INFORMATION...

I CAN TAKE IT...

I...

HIS HEART WOULD SURELY FAIL WERE HE TO HEAR THE WHOLE STORY.

HAH! JUST TWO WORDS AND *LOOK* AT HIM.

Gasp Pant Wheeze

HOLD IT!!

GETTING MARR—

THE COACH AND THE MANAGER ARE FINALLY...

IT IS WHAT WE WOULD LIKE TO BELIEVE.

IS THERE?

I KNOW YOU GUYS — THERE'S A CATCH SOMEWHERE, ISN'T THERE?

"OH, YOU'VE ALREADY HEARD? HOW EMBARRASSING!"

AHEM... "I SAY, MS. OTONASHI – I HEARD YOU'RE GETTING MARRIED TO SHUN MITAKA."

ALAS, NO. IT IS MERELY THAT, SO FAR, THERE HAS BEEN A GREAT RELUCTANCE TO CONFIRM THE FACTS.

THEN... THEN IT'S JUST MORE OF YOUR RUMORS?

ESPECIALLY IN *YOUR* CASE.

INDEED, WHAT RESPONSE COULD THERE BE?

IF SHE SAID THAT, WHAT WOULD *YOU* SAY, KID? *HUH?*

IMAGINE ME TO BE THE DIGNIFIED KYOKO OTONASHI...

......

YOU'VE BEEN AWFULLY QUIET FOR THE LAST FEW DAYS...

UM... MRS. ICHINOSE, IS THERE SOMETHING THE MATTER?

THERE'S JUST *GOT* TO BE SOME SORT OF MISTAKE.

IT... IT CAN'T BE.

EH?

ISN'T THERE SOMETHING... IMPORTANT... YOU'D LIKE TO TALK TO ME ABOUT?

LOOK...

140

OH, SHUN, HELLO!

HI, KYOKO SPEAKING.

RRIINNGG

I BETTER LEAVE — SEE YOU.

OH, GREAT!

YOU'VE DECIDED ON A WEDDING HALL? WHICH ONE?

JUST WHEN YOU THINK YOU KNOW A PERSON...

PSST

CLATTER

141

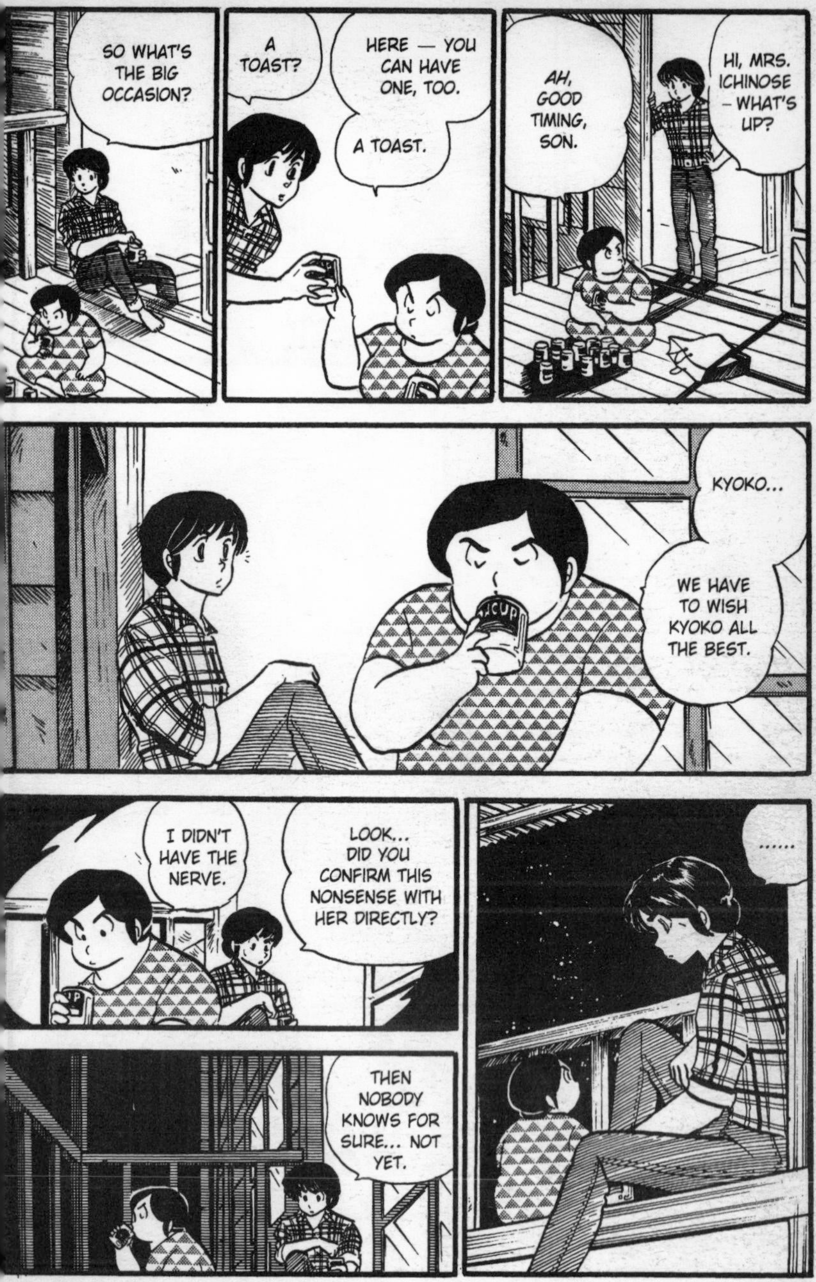
HI, MRS. ICHINOSE – WHAT'S UP?
AH, GOOD TIMING, SON.
HERE — YOU CAN HAVE ONE, TOO.
A TOAST.
A TOAST?
SO WHAT'S THE BIG OCCASION?
KYOKO...
WE HAVE TO WISH KYOKO ALL THE BEST.
LOOK... DID YOU CONFIRM THIS NONSENSE WITH HER DIRECTLY?
I DIDN'T HAVE THE NERVE.
THEN NOBODY KNOWS FOR SURE... NOT YET.
......

NO ONE TRIED TO FIND OUT THE TRUTH OF THIS RUMOR...

...THEY WERE ALL AFRAID TO.

...FIND OUT FOR MYSELF.

I MUST...

BUT I...

THANKS FOR HELPING ME OUT WITH ALL THE ARRANGEMENTS, KYOKO.

OH, DON'T WORRY ABOUT IT.

I JUST HOPE I WAS THE RIGHT CHOICE FOR YOU, THAT'S ALL.

BUT I'M SURE SHE WON'T LOOK EVEN HALF AS BEAUTIFUL AS *YOU* WOULD...

YEAH...

STILL — IT'LL ALL BE WORTH IT WHEN YOU SEE YOUR SISTER LOOKING SO BEAUTIFUL IN HER WEDDING GOWN!

I DIDN'T HAVE A CLUE WHAT TO... WEDDINGS ARE A COMPLETE MYSTERY TO ME.

YOU WERE A HUGE HELP.

WELL, THEY *CAN* BE A BIT DIFFICULT TO ARRANGE.

· · · ·

· · · ·

KANG KANG KANG KANG

AND IF IT *IS* TRUE...

THEN... THEN WHAT?

I'VE GOT TO MAKE SURE.

GOT TO HEAR IT FROM HER OWN LIPS.

YUSAKU...?

WELL, YES... I WAS WITH SHUN.

BEEN OUT SOME-WHERE?

...YOU'VE ALREADY HEARD?

OH...

...GOING TO BE A... W-WEDDING?

I-IS THERE...

GULP...

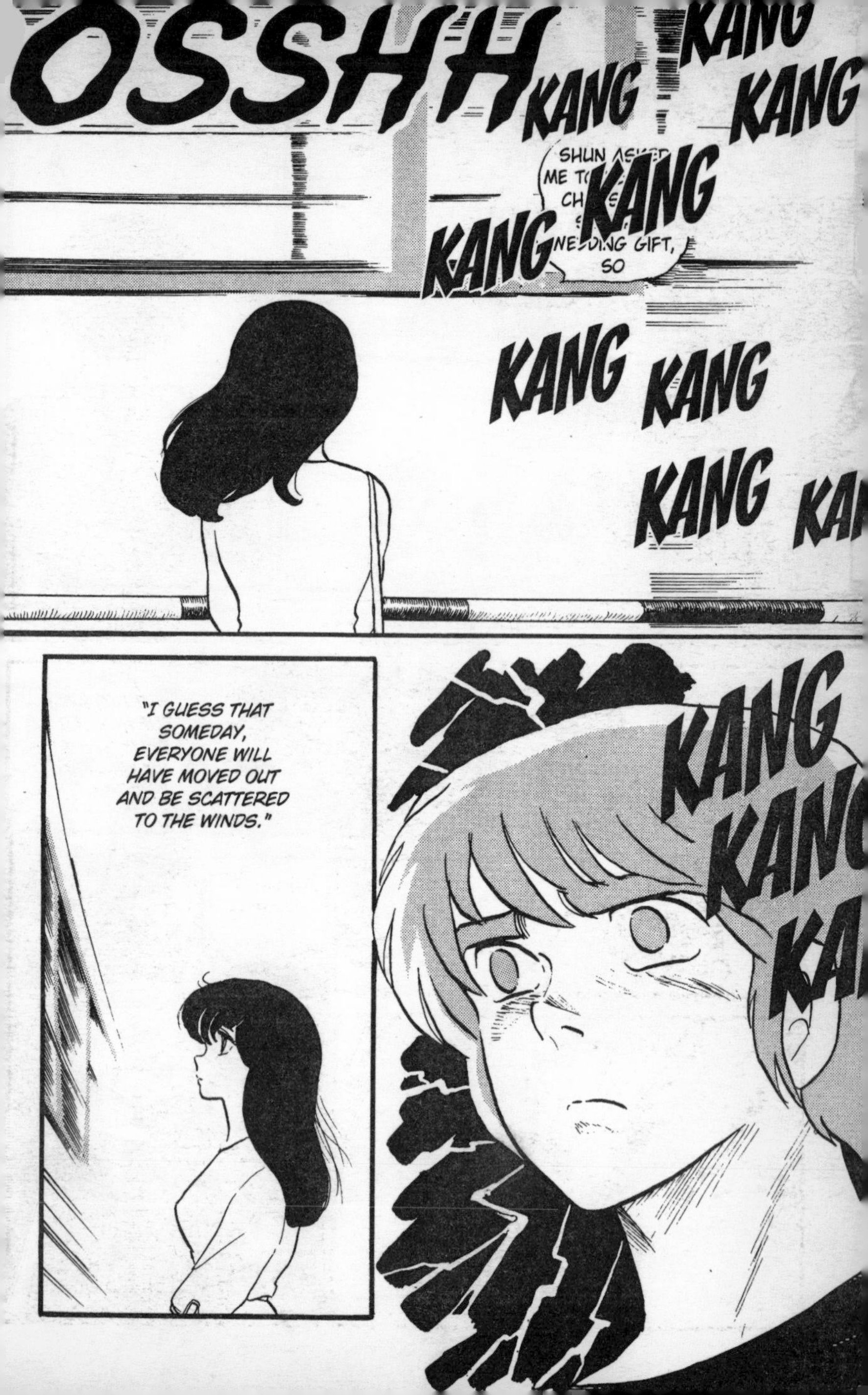
OSSHH
KANG KANG KANG KANG
SHUN
GIFT, SO
KANG KANG
KANG KANG KANG
KANG
"I GUESS THAT SOMEDAY, EVERYONE WILL HAVE MOVED OUT AND BE SCATTERED TO THE WINDS."

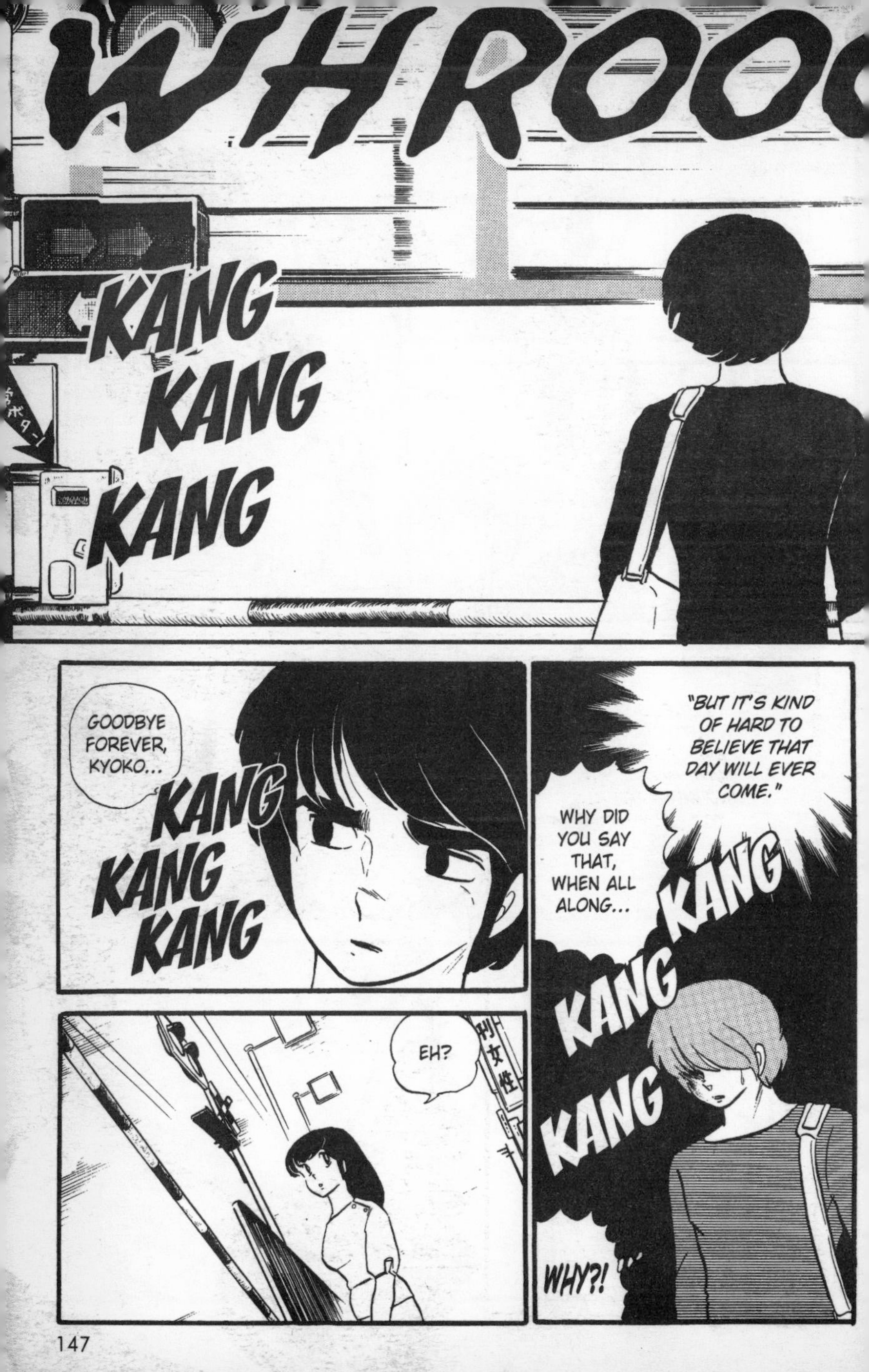
WHROOO
KANG
KANG
KANG
"BUT IT'S KIND OF HARD TO BELIEVE THAT DAY WILL EVER COME."
WHY DID YOU SAY THAT, WHEN ALL ALONG...
KANG
KANG
KANG
WHY?!
GOODBYE FOREVER, KYOKO...
KANG
KANG
KANG
EH?

"GOODBYE..." SOMETHING OR OTHER...

I WONDER WHAT HE SAID?

YUSAKU...?

...YOU IDIOT.

D-DON'T CRY...

SHKK

C'MON... YOU'RE NOT SERIOUS?

......

AND SO HE QUIETLY WITHDRAWS WITHOUT A FIGHT.

WHAT A WIMP.

LOOK, MS. OTONASHI KNEW HOW... HOW I FELT.

IF SHE KNEW AND STILL CHOSE MITAKA...

I'LL SEND A MOVING COMPANY TO PICK UP THE REST OF MY STUFF LATER.

I DON'T KNOW...

...BUT I CAN'T STAND TO BE HERE ANY LONGER, THAT'S ALL.

BUT WHEREVER WILL YOU GO?

WELL, YEAH... THAT'S TRUE, I GUESS...

...THEN WHAT POINT IS THERE IN PUTTING UP A FIGHT?

I'M HOME...

YEAH... WAY, *WAY* OUT.

UM... ARE YOU GOING OUT?

HM...?

I... I CAN'T SAY CONGRAT-ULATIONS...

MS. OTO-NASHI...

...BUT I HOPE YOU'LL BE HAPPY.

I'M SICK OF MYSELF AND MY LIFE.

WHY ARE YOU—

YUSAKU, *WHAT* IS GOING ON HERE?!

WHAT—?

WAIT!

THANKS FOR EVERY-THING... IT WAS NICE KNOWING YOU.

...TIME TO LOOK INSIDE MY HEART.

I NEED SOME TIME ALONE...

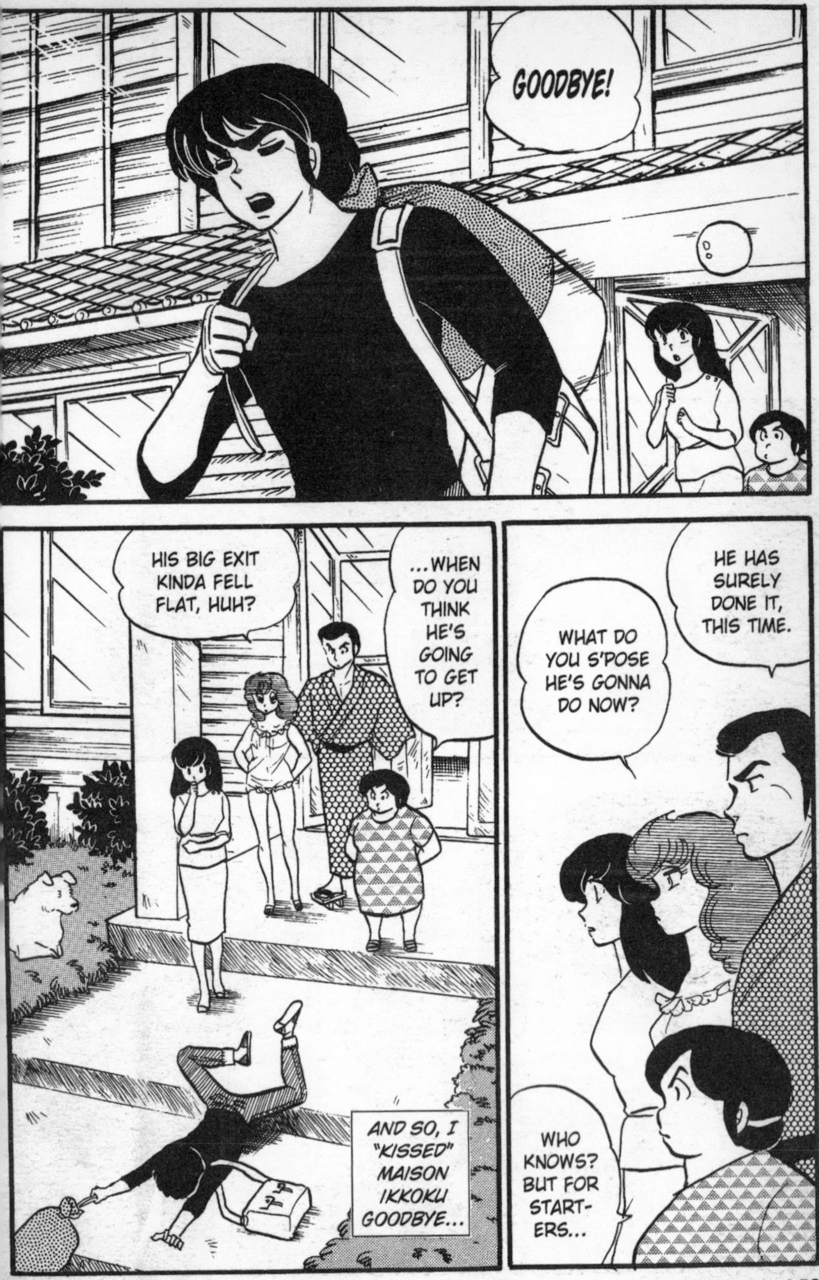
GOODBYE!
HIS BIG EXIT KINDA FELL FLAT, HUH?
...WHEN DO YOU THINK HE'S GOING TO GET UP?
AND SO, I "KISSED" MAISON IKKOKU GOODBYE...
HE HAS SURELY DONE IT, THIS TIME.
WHAT DO YOU S'POSE HE'S GONNA DO NOW?
WHO KNOWS? BUT FOR STARTERS...

PART EIGHT
A SMALL SPACE

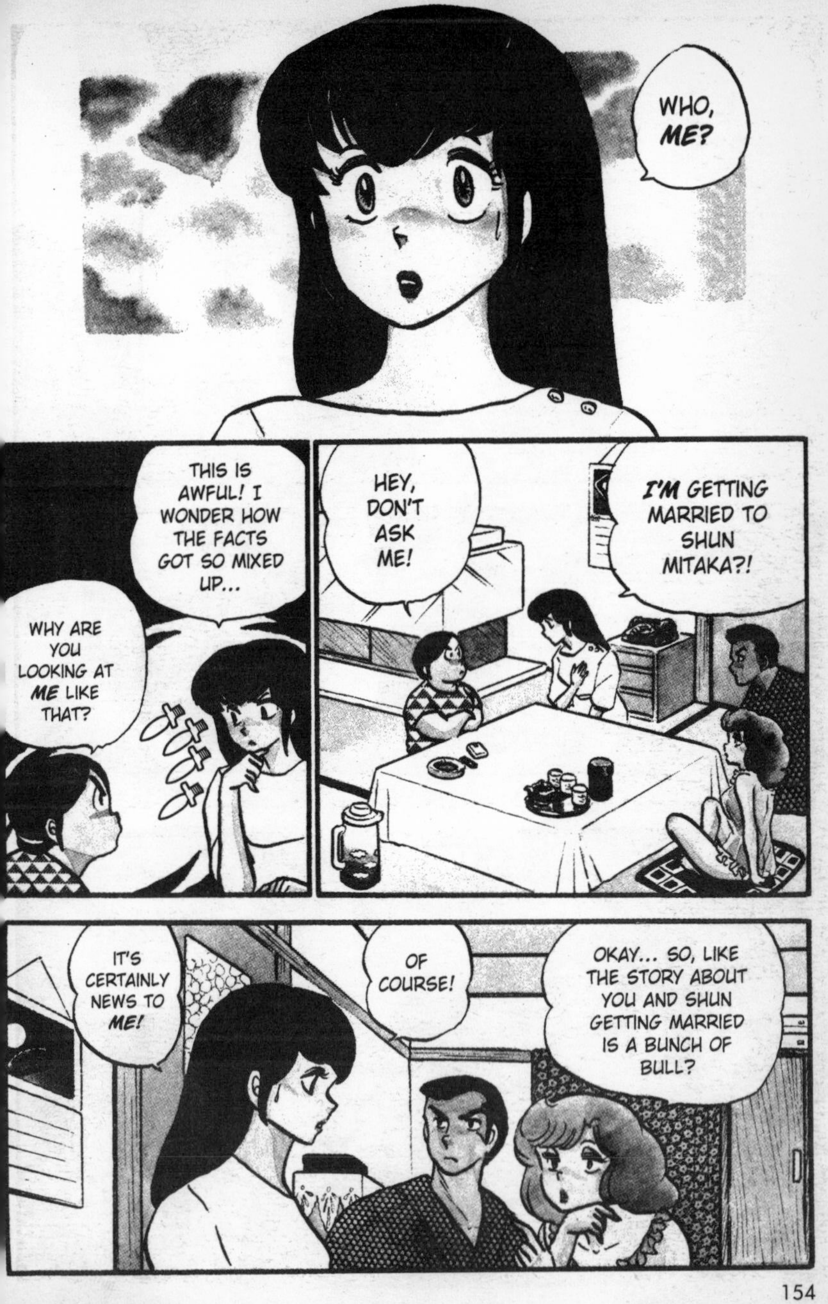

WHO, *ME?*
I'M GETTING MARRIED TO SHUN MITAKA?!
HEY, DON'T ASK ME!
THIS IS AWFUL! I WONDER HOW THE FACTS GOT SO MIXED UP...
WHY ARE YOU LOOKING AT *ME* LIKE THAT?
OKAY... SO, LIKE THE STORY ABOUT YOU AND SHUN GETTING MARRIED IS A BUNCH OF BULL?
OF COURSE!
IT'S CERTAINLY NEWS TO *ME!*

I JUST *CAN'T* IMAGINE HOW THIS STORY GOT SO WARPED...!

I WAS JUST HELPING HIM PICK OUT A PRESENT FOR HER, THAT'S ALL.

THE PERSON GETTING MARRIED ISN'T *ME*, IT'S SHUN'S YOUNGER SISTER!!

IT IS SAID, "WHERE THERE'S SMOKE, THERE'S FIRE."

UH... ER... DON'T *WE* HAVE MORE IMPORTANT THINGS TO TALK ABOUT?

YUSAKU ISN'T A *DOG*, MR. YOTSUYA!

PERHAPS HE WILL RETURN TO HIS HOME WHEN HE GETS HUNGRY...?

WITH *HIM*? NOT MUCH.

SO WHAT ARE WE GOING TO DO?

I MEAN, YUSAKU PACKED UP AND LEFT BECAUSE OF THIS MESS.

RIGHT, JUST SIGN THERE, AND THERE.

THE NEXT DAY...

I'VE GOTTA SAY, YOU'RE ONE LUCKY YOUNG MAN.

CHING

SO I FOUND A NEW PLACE RIGHT AWAY.

BY SIGNING, I TRULY SEVERED MY TIES TO MAISON IKKOKU.

YEAH...

YOU HARDLY EVER SEE ONE SO NEAR THE STATION FOR ONLY ¥20,000.

THIS APARTMENT WAS JUST LISTED THIS MORNING.

I TELL YA, KID — YOU'RE DAMN LUCKY.

FOR ONE THING, I'M THROUGH WITH WOMEN!

THIS IS MY CHANCE TO REALLY CHANGE MY LIFE... TO FIND MYSELF.

MUST BE IT.

"SECOND FLOOR OF THE SUPER SPACE PACHINKO PARLOR"...

ching ching

chingg
tiktiktik
shrakkk
ching ching

HUH?

NOT LOCKED?

KCHAK

Shrakkk ching

KREEK

GURK!

KREE

W-W-WRONG DOOR!

S-S-SORRY!!

HMM?

...?

SLAM

LESSEE... "CLOCK HILL STATION WEST, SECOND FLOOR OF THE SUPER SPACE PACHINKO PARLOR, APARTMENT 1"...

JEEZ, WHAT A SURPRISE!

YOU AGAIN?

ER...

COME IN!

THIS *IS* NUMBER 1...

WELL, *UH,* ACTUALLY, IT'S ABOUT THAT...

MOVING OUT, I MEAN.

LOOK, IF YOU'RE TRYING TO GET ME TO SUBSCRIBE TO THE PAPER...

...YOU'RE WASTING YOUR TIME. I'M MOVING OUT SOON.

WELL, *RATS!*

THEY *ALREADY* FOUND SOMEONE?

HUH?

I, *UH,* I JUST RENTED THIS PLACE TODAY... I'M SUPPOSED TO MOVE IN RIGHT AWAY.

I MEAN, I'VE ALREADY SIGNED THE LEASE AND EVERYTHING!

YOU THINK *YOU'VE* GOT A PAIN?

WELL, THEN, I GUESS IT'S YOUR PLACE NOW!

"DELAYED"?! WHAT?!

...'CAUSE MY PLANS TO MOVE HAVE BEEN KINDA DELAYED.

THAT'S A REAL PAIN...

I DON'T HAVE ANYPLACE ELSE TO GO, EITHER!

...SO I COULDN'T MOVE EVEN IF I HAD TO!

BUT I DON'T HAVE ANY MONEY...

I'VE GOT IT!

HEY!

SOUNDS LIKE WE HAVE A PROBLEM, ALL RIGHT.

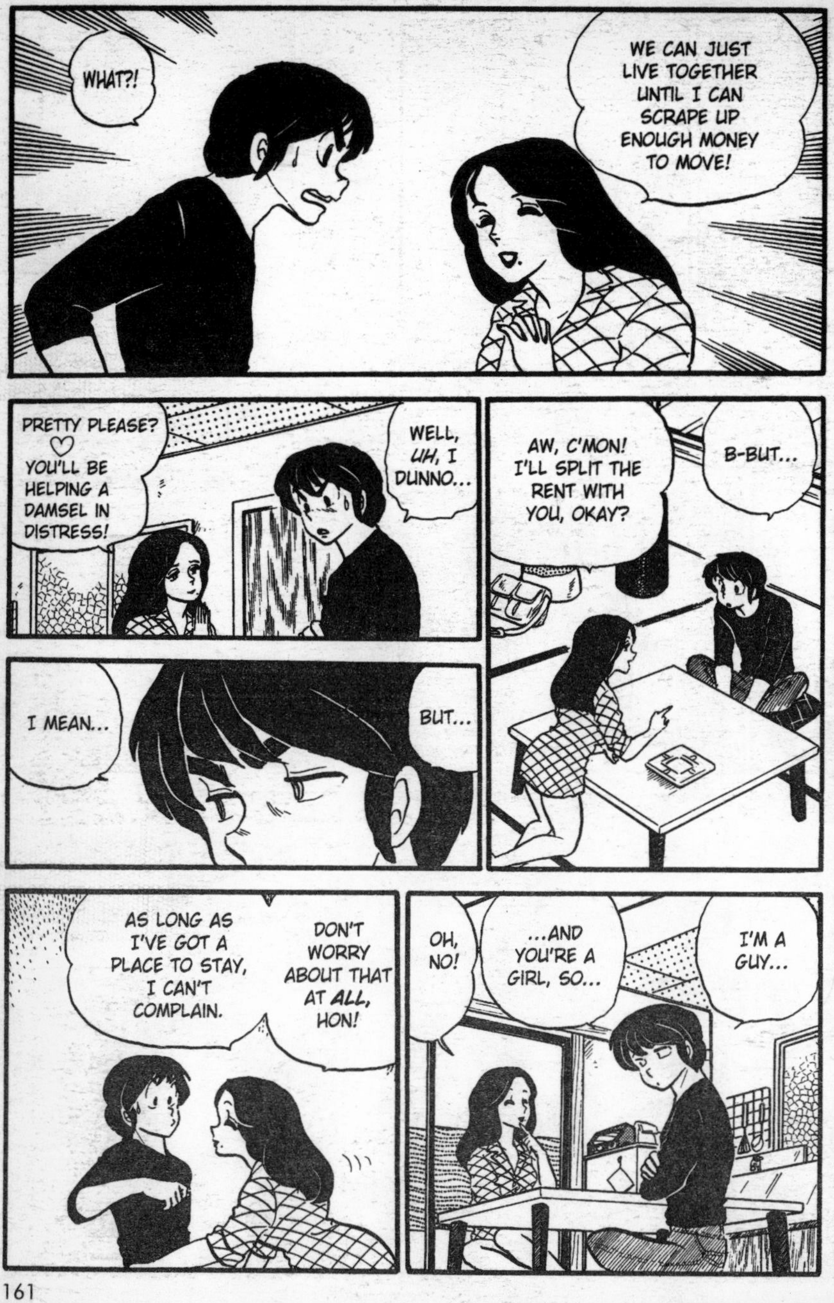
WE CAN JUST LIVE TOGETHER UNTIL I CAN SCRAPE UP ENOUGH MONEY TO MOVE!
WHAT?!
B-BUT...
AW, C'MON! I'LL SPLIT THE RENT WITH YOU, OKAY?
WELL, *UH*, I DUNNO...
PRETTY PLEASE? ♡ YOU'LL BE HELPING A DAMSEL IN DISTRESS!
BUT...
I MEAN...
I'M A GUY...
...AND YOU'RE A GIRL, SO...
OH, NO!
DON'T WORRY ABOUT THAT AT *ALL*, HON!
AS LONG AS I'VE GOT A PLACE TO STAY, I CAN'T COMPLAIN.

WELL, UH...

ulp!

RIGHT?

AND IT'S GOING TO HELP BOTH OF US OUT, RIGHT?

I MEAN, WE'D ONLY BE "LIVING IN SIN" FOR A WEEK OR TWO.

ALL *RIGHT!*

I GUESS... IF IT'S OKAY WITH YOU...

SO, YOU GOING TO COLLEGE?

GOTTA BE SOME BEER IN HERE...

WHAT'S YOUR NAME?

HUH?

LET'S HAVE A DRINK TO CELEBRATE, OKAY?

...THIS REMINDS ME OF MAISON IKKOKU.

JEEZ...

UH, CHEERS.

KANK

CHEERS!

I'M *AYAKO.* PLEASED T'MEETCHA!

WHEN I FIRST MOVED IN THERE...

AS SOON AS I GET ENOUGH MONEY, I'M OUTTA HERE.

AH, WELL.

MAN, WHAT A GRUBBY LITTLE APARTMENT.

??

skritch skritch skritch

163

GREETINGS.

AIEE!

WHAM

I AM YOTSUYA, FROM ROOM 4.

W-WHO ARE YOU?!

CHEERS!

ALL RIGHT, A ROOM-WARMING PARTY! LET'S DRINK!

THUD THUD

......

HEY, KID, I HEAR YOU'RE A FLUNK-OUT!

THUD THUD

THE ONLY REASON I STAYED IN THAT MADHOUSE WAS BECAUSE OF HER...

BWA HA HA

I HAVEN'T EVEN UNPACKED YET!

WAIT! HOLD ON A DAMN SECOND!

DAMN IT, WHAT AM I THINKING?

...BECAUSE KYOKO WAS THERE.

THE REASON I LEFT THERE WITHOUT EVEN TAKING MY STUFF WAS TO MAKE A CLEAN BREAK.

KYOKO...

I'M... THROUGH WITH WOMEN...

YOU SEEM KINDA SAD...

SOME-THING WRONG, HON?

I'M *THROUGH* WITH WOMEN!

BINK

HEARD FROM YUSAKU?

...

NOT A WORD.

I SEE...

MAYBE...

IT'S JUST...

YOU WORRIED?

166

WELL, I JUST DON'T WANT THINGS TO END THIS WAY.

I WANT HIM TO KNOW THE TRUTH.

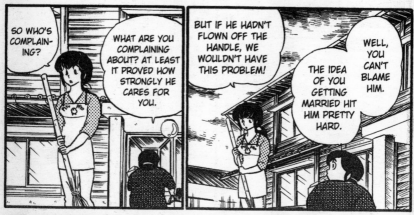

SO WHO'S COMPLAINING?

WHAT ARE YOU COMPLAINING ABOUT? AT LEAST IT PROVED HOW STRONGLY HE CARES FOR YOU.

BUT IF HE HADN'T FLOWN OFF THE HANDLE, WE WOULDN'T HAVE THIS PROBLEM!

WELL, YOU CAN'T BLAME HIM.

THE IDEA OF YOU GETTING MARRIED HIT HIM PRETTY HARD.

THAT... THAT WIMP!

HE GIVES UP TOO EASILY!

167

WELL...

SO WHAT DO YOU DO FOR A LIVING?

ER... AYAKO...

......

TODAY'S MY DAY OFF.

I WORK AT A MASSAGE PARLOR.

LET'S EAT!

SOUP'S ON!

AT A *MASSAGE PARLOR?!?*

SO SHE'S A...

HERE...

168

 UH... THERE'S PLENTY, IF YOU WANT MORE.

 I CAN'T TASTE A THING.

YOU BET!

 TASTY...?

 WE ARE? I MEAN, SURE.

HUH?

SINCE WE'RE SPLITTING THE FOOD EXPENSES, TOO, IT'S A WASTE IF YOU DON'T EAT.

 This is channel 12, live from this extraordinary demonstration...

 ...as you can see, thousands of candles...

...

169

MAYBE SHE'S EXPECTING ME TO...

STILL, MAYBE...

SHE SURE SEEMS RELAXED AROUND ME. MAYBE...

NAW, NO WAY.

I WONDER WHAT KIND OF GIRL SHE IS.

...for world peace...

More!

WHAT ARE YOU THINKING, YOU MORON?!

YOU JUST GOT YOUR HEART BROKEN YESTERDAY!

I'LL GET THE FUTON READY.

YOU MIND FOLDING UP THE TABLE, HON?

Y-YEAH, SURE!

GETTING LATE... TIME FOR BED, MM?

IT... IT'S FINALLY GOING TO HAPPEN...

...TO ME!

YOU MUST BE TIRED AFTER MOVING.

YOU OUGHT TO COME TO BED, TOO.

D... DON'T LOOK AT ME LIKE THAT!

YOU'RE THE ONE WHO LEFT ME.

YUSAKU...

...

...

MM?

SOME-THING WRONG, HON?

WELCOME HOME!

HI, HONEY!

HEY, BABE, LOVER BOY'S BACK!!

URK?

WHY... YOU...

...

...

172

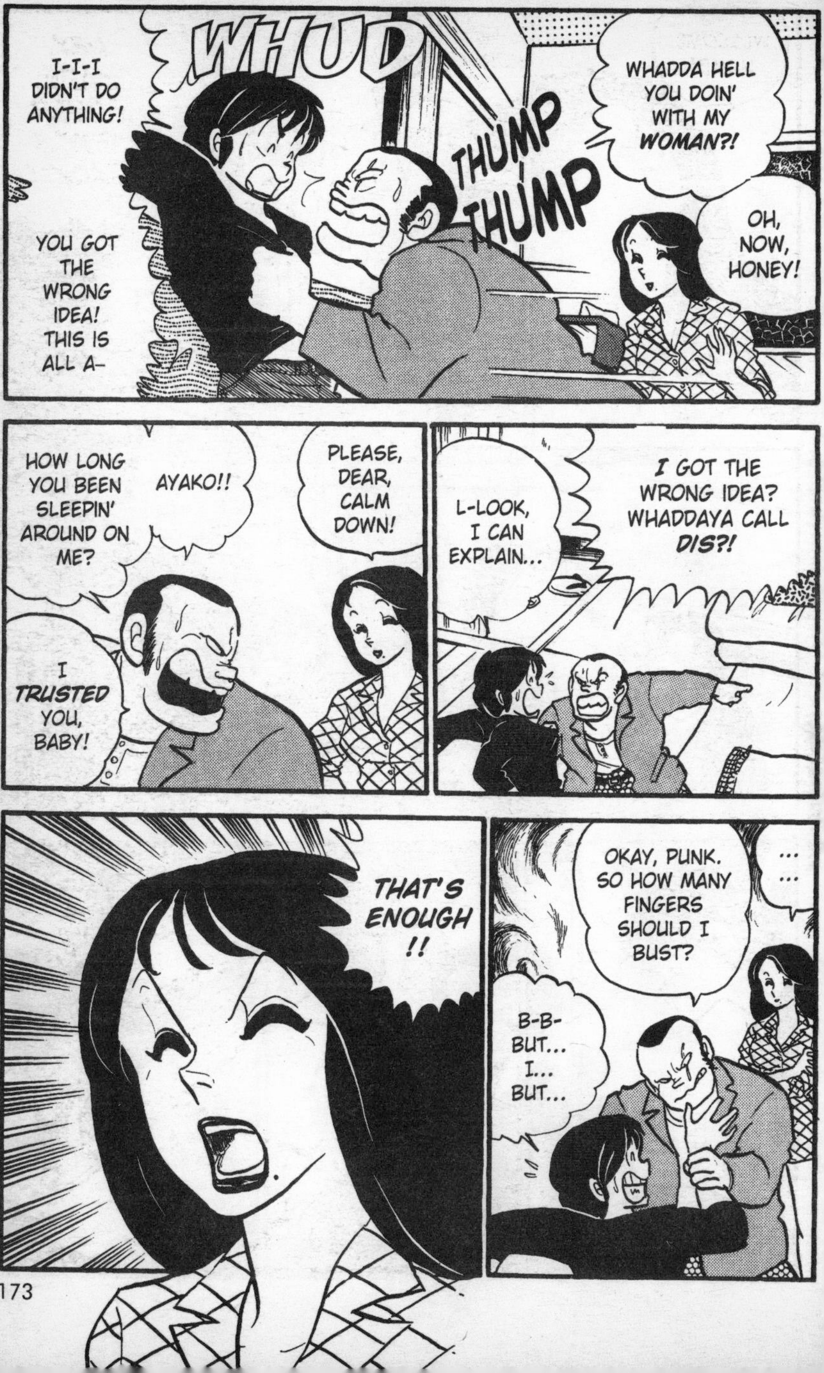
WHUD
I-I-I DIDN'T DO ANYTHING!
YOU GOT THE WRONG IDEA! THIS IS ALL A-
THUMP THUMP
WHADDA HELL YOU DOIN' WITH MY WOMAN?!
OH, NOW, HONEY!
I GOT THE WRONG IDEA? WHADDAYA CALL DIS?!
L-LOOK, I CAN EXPLAIN...
PLEASE, DEAR, CALM DOWN!
AYAKO!!
HOW LONG YOU BEEN SLEEPIN' AROUND ON ME?
I TRUSTED YOU, BABY!
......
OKAY, PUNK. SO HOW MANY FINGERS SHOULD I BUST?
B-B-BUT... I... BUT...
THAT'S ENOUGH!!

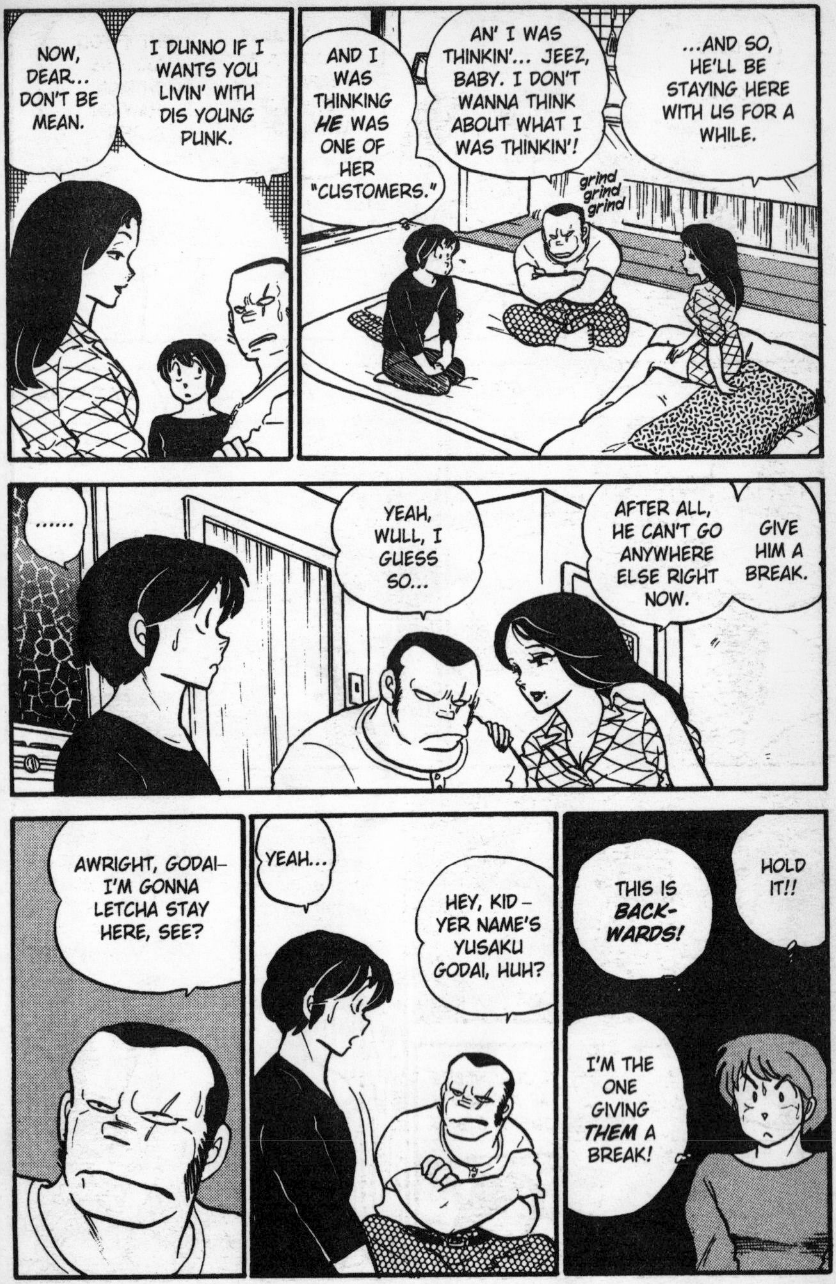
...AND SO, HE'LL BE STAYING HERE WITH US FOR A WHILE.
AN' I WAS THINKIN'... JEEZ, BABY. I DON'T WANNA THINK ABOUT WHAT I WAS THINKIN'!
grind grind grind
AND I WAS THINKING *HE* WAS ONE OF HER "CUSTOMERS."
I DUNNO IF I WANTS YOU LIVIN' WITH DIS YOUNG PUNK.
NOW, DEAR... DON'T BE MEAN.
AFTER ALL, HE CAN'T GO ANYWHERE ELSE RIGHT NOW.
GIVE HIM A BREAK.
YEAH, WULL, I GUESS SO...
......
AWRIGHT, GODAI- I'M GONNA LETCHA STAY HERE, SEE?
YEAH...
HEY, KID- YER NAME'S YUSAKU GODAI, HUH?
HOLD IT!!
THIS IS *BACKWARDS!*
I'M THE ONE GIVING *THEM* A BREAK!

LOUD AND CLEAR.

YOU AIN'T GONNA BE *USIN'* THAT PAW FOR A WHILE. GET IT?

BUT IF YOU LAY ONE STINKIN' PAW ON AYAKO...

OH, REALLY, HONEY!

I GOTTA GET US SOME MORE DOUGH.

OH, YEAH... *DAT*...

BY THE WAY, DEAR, DID YOU GET OUR MOVING MONEY?

YOU LOST IT ALL, DIDN'T YOU?

ON THE HORSES.

WELL, YA KNOW WE NEEDED T'REE TIMES DAT MUCH T' MOVE, SEE?

YEAH, DAT.

WHAT HAPPENED TO ALL THE MONEY YOU HAD THIS MORNING?

I JUS' NEEDS ME A STAKE... JUS' A STAKE.

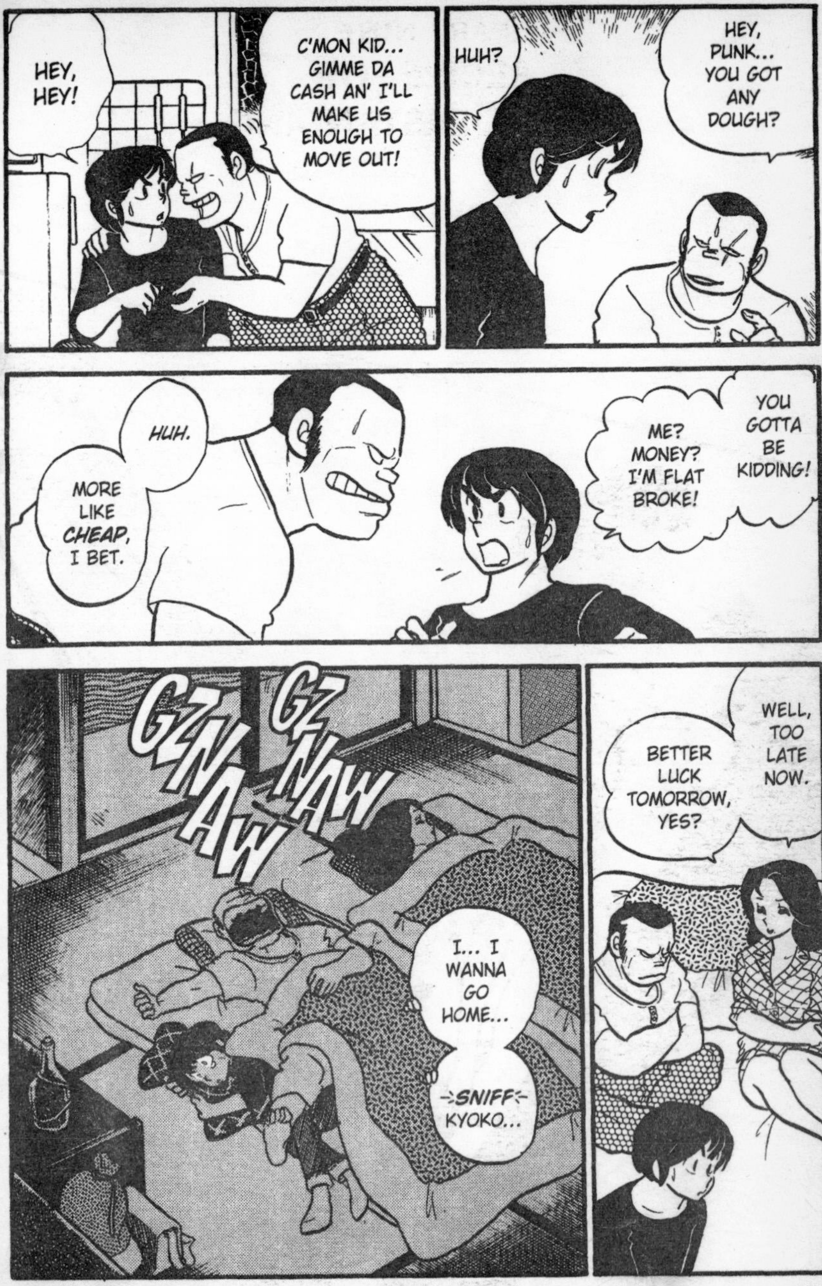
HEY, PUNK... YOU GOT ANY DOUGH?
HUH?
HEY, HEY!
C'MON KID... GIMME DA CASH AN' I'LL MAKE US ENOUGH TO MOVE OUT!
YOU GOTTA BE KIDDING!
ME? MONEY? I'M FLAT BROKE!
HUH.
MORE LIKE *CHEAP*, I BET.
WELL, TOO LATE NOW.
BETTER LUCK TOMORROW, YES?
GZ NAW
GZNAW
I... I WANNA GO HOME...
-SNIFF- KYOKO...

PART NINE
RECIPE FOR MISUNDERSTANDING

JUST SIGN HERE, MA'AM.

THANKS.

BRMBBBB

SO *NOW* WHAT DO I DO?

GUESS HE DIDN'T EVEN TELL HIS PARENTS THAT HE'D MOVED.

IT'S FOR YUSAKU...

...

VROOM

MAISON IKKOKU

....

....

FWIP

OH, HI, MR. YOTSUYA— WHERE ARE YOU GOING?

I AM GOING OUT.

I'M NOT HIDING IT... REALLY...

WHY DO YOU CONCEAL IT?

IT'S *NOT* FOR YOU.

A PACKAGE, IS IT NOT?

AH, I SEE IT IS FOR YOUNG GODAI.

GIVE ME A BREAK — IF THERE'S FOOD IN THERE, YOU'LL EAT IT, ALL RIGHT!

I ASSURE YOU THAT I DO NOT PLAN TO CONSUME THE CONTENTS.

I DON'T THINK SO!

I WILL TAKE CARE OF IT UNTIL HIS RETURN.

OUR MANAGER IS CASTING ASPERSIONS UPON MY CHARACTER.

NOTHING, MRS. ICHINOSE.

WHAT ARE YOU TWO UP TO OUT HERE?

I WONDER IF HE REALLY PLANS TO MOVE OUT PERMANENTLY.

YES, AND I CAN'T EVEN FORWARD IT TO HIM, SINCE I DON'T KNOW HIS NEW ADDRESS.

A PACKAGE FOR YUSAKU, EH?

THAT'S TRUE.

AFTER ALL, ALL HIS JUNK IS STILL IN HIS ROOM.

YOU SHOULDN'T EVEN *THINK* SUCH THINGS, MRS. ICHINOSE! HONESTLY!

HEY, MAYBE HE JUMPED OFF A BRIDGE OR SOMETHING!

EVEN SO, IT HAS BEEN ALMOST AN ENTIRE MONTH.

I DON'T THINK YOU GET IT!! IT'S BEEN A *MONTH!!*

CHING!! TIKTIKTIK

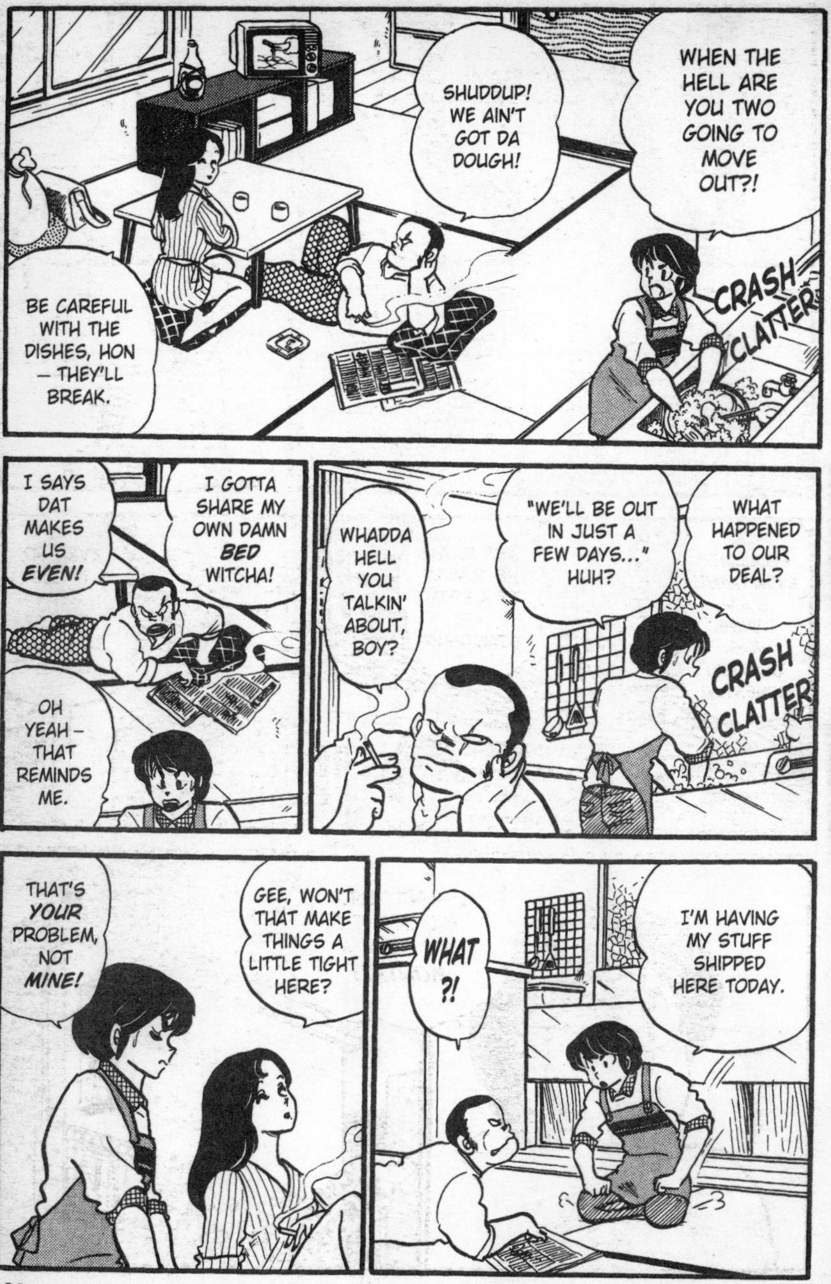
WHEN THE HELL ARE YOU TWO GOING TO MOVE OUT?!
CRASH CLATTER
SHUDDUP! WE AIN'T GOT DA DOUGH!
BE CAREFUL WITH THE DISHES, HON — THEY'LL BREAK.
WHAT HAPPENED TO OUR DEAL?
"WE'LL BE OUT IN JUST A FEW DAYS..." HUH?
CRASH CLATTER
WHADDA HELL YOU TALKIN' ABOUT, BOY?
I GOTTA SHARE MY OWN DAMN BED WITCHA!
I SAYS DAT MAKES US EVEN!
OH YEAH — THAT REMINDS ME.
I'M HAVING MY STUFF SHIPPED HERE TODAY.
WHAT ?!
GEE, WON'T THAT MAKE THINGS A LITTLE TIGHT HERE?
THAT'S YOUR PROBLEM, NOT MINE!

YOU KNOW, I KIND OF HAD THE SAME FEELING MYSELF.

YOU GUYS ACT LIKE I'M YOUR KID OR SOMETHING!!

NOW, DEAR, YOU'RE DREAMING AGAIN.

I'LL DOUBLE IT FER YUH!

GIMME DAT DOUGH!

DEN WE'LL HAVE ENUFF TO *MOVE* ON, AN' YOU'LL GET SOME EXTRA, HEY?

SAY, SON... YOU GOT SOME CASH FER TH' MOVERS,

NOW WHAT?

BUT IF HE COMES TO THE PARLOR, HE'LL JUST BE ANOTHER CUSTOMER, RIGHT?

DAMN IT AYAKO, YOU AIN'T GONNA... WIT DAT *KID*?

I'LL SHOW YOU A *REAL* GOOD TIME, HON.

WHAT YOU SHOULD DO IS COME TO MY MASSAGE PARLOR WITH THAT MONEY.

WHAT DO YOU MEAN, "FAMILY"?!

AND THE MONEY WOULD JUST END UP RIGHT BACK IN THE FAMILY, SO IT'S A WIN-WIN DEAL, MM?

I CAN STAKE OUT A CLAIM FOR SOME FLOOR SPACE.

ANYWAY, ONCE I MOVE IN MY FURNITURE...

I CAN'T BELIEVE THOSE PEOPLE!

DAMN IT ALL!

...IT'S REALLY GOODBYE, ISN'T IT?

ON THE OTHER HAND, ONCE I MOVE IT OUT OF MAISON IKKOKU...

I WONDER IF SHE'S OKAY...

KYOKO...

SPARKLE SMILE

RRG!

WELL, SHE'S NOT MY CONCERN ANYMORE.

BECAUSE SHE BELONGS TO THAT DAMNED MITAKA NOW.

I'M SUCH AN IDIOT...

CHUG CHUG CHUG

CHUG CHUG

ANYBODY HOME...?

BUT HE LEFT ALL HIS STUFF...

...SO MAYBE...

CHUG CHUG CHUG

MAYBE I OUGHT TO JUST SEND IT BACK...

PIYO

WHERE'S ROOM 5?

WE'RE THE MOVERS.

YES?

HUH... LOOKS LIKE THE KID *WAS* SERIOUS, AFTER ALL.

THUD THUD

......

PIYO PIYO

UMM, EXCUSE ME...

WE'RE ALL DONE HERE, MA'AM — THANKS!

WHY, THAT'S JUST THE NEXT STATION OVER.

CLOCK HILL WEST...

I... *UH*... SORT OF MISPLACED IT.

COULD YOU GIVE ME HIS NEW ADDRESS?

SURE, NO PROBLEM.

MAYBE... MAYBE I SHOULD HAVE JUST GIVEN IT TO THE MOVERS...

KLIK

VOOSH VROOSH

SIGH...

YOU DIDN'T EVEN BOTHER TO ASK *ME* ABOUT IT.

YOU DIDN'T HAVE TO GO, YOU KNOW.

SOMETIMES YOU'RE SUCH A FOOL.

HNNG... THERE'S NO ROOM, NO ROOM...

GZNAWW SNZZZ

I WONDER HOW HE'S DOING NOW...

...
...

RIGHT?

WELL, I CAN'T KEEP THIS FOREVER.

Pito

ASK ME IF I CARE.

IT'S ALL YER DAMN CRAP! I DIDN'T GET A WINK UH SLEEP!

DAMN IT, I AIN'T DOIN' SO GOOD TODAY.

KRAK KRIK

KRIK

TOUGH LUCK – I JUST RAN OUT.

HEY, KID, GIMME SOME BALLS.

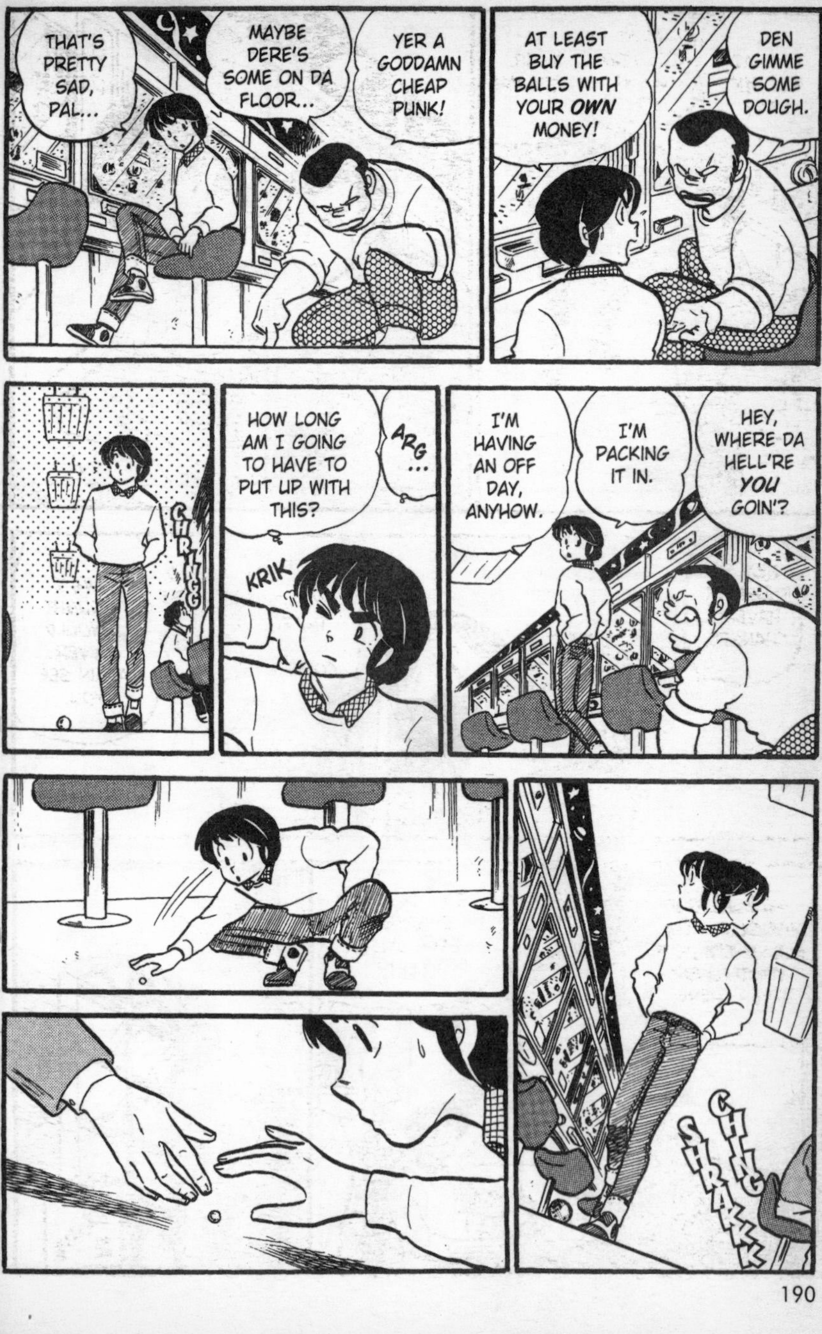
THAT'S PRETTY SAD, PAL...
MAYBE DERE'S SOME ON DA FLOOR...
YER A GODDAMN CHEAP PUNK!
AT LEAST BUY THE BALLS WITH YOUR *OWN* MONEY!
DEN GIMME SOME DOUGH.
CHRING
HOW LONG AM I GOING TO HAVE TO PUT UP WITH THIS?
ARG...
KRIK
HEY, WHERE DA HELL'RE *YOU* GOIN'?
I'M PACKING IT IN.
I'M HAVING AN OFF DAY, ANYHOW.
CHING
SHRAKKK

IS THAT NOT *MY* LINE?

WHAT ARE *YOU* DOING HERE?

M-MR. YOTSUYA!

NICE TO KNOW YOU HAVEN'T CHANGED.

YOUR TREAT, OF COURSE.

WOULD YOU LIKE A COFFEE?

AHH, I THOUGHT I WOULD NEVER AGAIN SEE YOU.

AH, EVERYONE HAS BEEN WELL. INDEED, IT'S AS IF YOU'D NEVER LIVED THERE.

SO... HOW HAS EVERYBODY BEEN SINCE I LEFT?

HAS... *UH*... HAS IT BEEN SET?

UH...

THE DATE, I MEAN.

QUITE SO.

NO KIDDING...

I WASN'T TALKING ABOUT *YOU*, DUMMY!

I FAIL TO UNDERSTAND — I HAVE NO PLANS FOR MARRIAGE.

...OF THE W-WEDDING.

OF THE...

DATE OF THE WHAT?

A...

...RUMOR?

OH, THAT.

I'M TALKING ABOUT THE WEDDING BETWEEN KYOKO AND THAT DAMN TENNIS COACH!

HUH?

FEAR NOT, THAT WAS NOTHING MORE THAN A RUMOR.

BUT DON'T CONCERN YOURSELF.

......

YOU ACTED MOST PRECIPITOUSLY, YOUNG GODAI.

IF ONLY YOU HAD LISTENED CALMLY AND RATIONALLY TO THE ENTIRE STORY...

......

EVERYONE AT MAISON IKKOKU HAS QUITE FORGOTTEN YOU, AND LIVES IN PEACE AND TRANQUILITY.

NOK NOK

KAN KAN KAN

SUPER SPACE PACHINKO...

THIS MUST BE IT.

193

HELLO?

SURE IS!

ER... THIS ISN'T YUSAKU GODAI'S ROOM, IS IT...?

I SEE...

I...

AYAKO... I'M LIVING HERE WITH YUSAKU.

UM, SORRY TO PRY, BUT JUST WHO ARE YOU?

194

...!

SHE DROPPED OFF THIS PACKAGE FOR YOU.

WHAT?! MY EX-LANDLADY WAS HERE?!

I HAVE TO APOLOGIZE TO HER FOR THIS WHOLE CRAZY MIX-UP!!

T.MP
T.MP
T.MP

YES, JUST A MINUTE AGO.

...TO MOVE BACK IN!

I MIGHT STILL HAVE A CHANCE...

AHA!

195

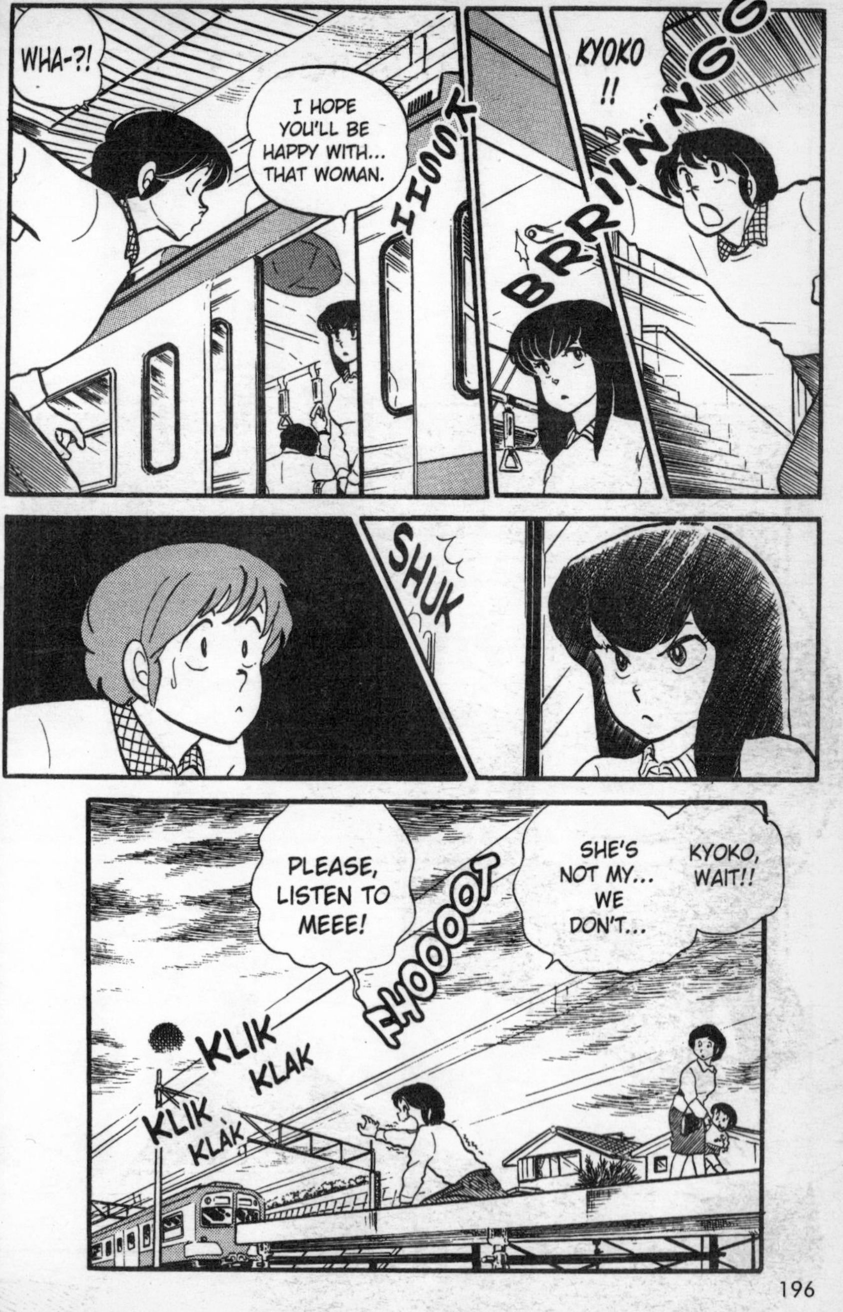
WHA-?!
I HOPE YOU'LL BE HAPPY WITH... THAT WOMAN.
HISSST
KYOKO !!
BRRIINNGG
SHUK
PLEASE, LISTEN TO MEEE!
FHOOOOT
SHE'S NOT MY... WE DON'T...
KYOKO, WAIT!!
KLIK KLAK
KLIK KLAK

PART TEN
THE LIGHT IN ROOM 5

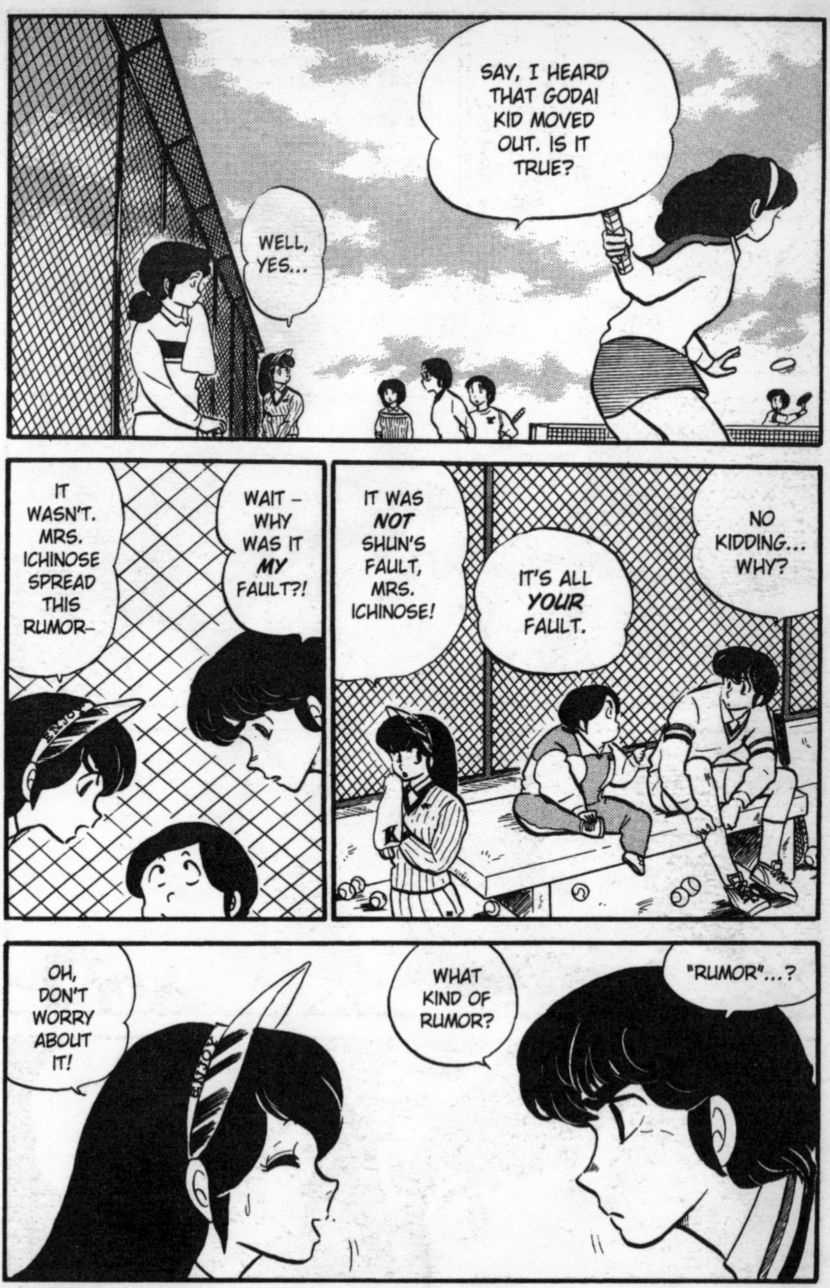

SAY, I HEARD THAT GODAI KID MOVED OUT. IS IT TRUE?
WELL, YES...
NO KIDDING... WHY?
IT'S ALL *YOUR* FAULT.
IT WAS *NOT* SHUN'S FAULT, MRS. ICHINOSE!
WAIT – WHY WAS IT *MY* FAULT?!
IT WASN'T. MRS. ICHINOSE SPREAD THIS RUMOR–
ENJOY
"RUMOR"...?
WHAT KIND OF RUMOR?
OH, DON'T WORRY ABOUT IT!
ENJOY

SO THEN HE JUST PULLED OUT OF THE COMPETITION?

YEP!

NO KIDDING.

WHAT DO YOU MEAN, "DON'T HAVE A CLUE HOW IT GOT STARTED" ...?

WELL... *UMM...* SOMEHOW, WORD GOT AROUND THAT THE TWO OF YOU WERE GETTING MARRIED. I DON'T HAVE A CLUE HOW IT GOT STARTED, THOUGH.

WELL, WELL, WELL...

C'MON... WITH THE COACH AS HIS RIVAL?

DON'T YOU THINK IT'S DISGUSTING THAT HE GAVE UP SO EASILY?

NOT UNTIL THE BITTER END...

IF I WERE HIM, I'D *NEVER* GIVE UP...

Making his move...

There he goes...

I'M LIVING HERE WITH YUSAKU...

......

HEY, HEY — YOU KNOW SOMETHING WE DON'T?

WELL, PERSONALLY, I DON'T THINK I WAS THE REASON FOR HIM MOVING OUT.

HE... UH.

WELL, I DON'T!

Y'KNOW, I THINK YOU *DO* KNOW SOMETHING.

...I'M NOT THE ONLY WOMAN IN THE WORLD.

IT'S TRUE...

"TIME ALONE"... HAH!

I NEED SOME TIME ALONE... TIME TO LOOK INSIDE MY HEART.

THE REASON HE LEFT JUST LIKE THAT...

...IS BECAUSE HE HAD *THAT WOMAN* ALREADY.

HELLO, KYOKO SPEAK-ING...

UH, KYOKO, THIS IS YUSAKU.

LOOK, I'VE GOTTA TELL YOU—

AW, KYOKO, DON'T HANG UP!!

HELLO? HELLO?!

......

YES – THEY NEVER SEEM TO GET THE MESSAGE.

SEEMS LIKE YOU'RE GETTING A LOT OF THOSE LATELY...

PRETTY MUCH.

WHAT WAS THAT? A PRANK CALL?

I *THOUGHT* SO. IT WAS WRITTEN ALL OVER YOUR FACE.

EH?!

IT'S YUSAKU, ISN'T IT?

ULP!

....

......

HE'S *NOT* ALONE!!

THAT'S NOT VERY NICE, KYOKO! HERE HE'S ALL ALONE AND DEPRESSED, AND YOU–

WHAT'S GOING ON?

YOU SURE GAVE HIM THE COLD SHOULDER.

BUT...

HE'S... NO KIDDING!

HE'S LIVING WITH SOME FLOOZY!

202

MAN, I WANNA MOVE BACK...

SHRAKK

CHINGG

KANG KANG

DUMB BROAD... SHE DIDN'T HAVE TO HANG UP ON ME LIKE THAT.

......

HYOOOOO

WOW, SUKIYAKI!

WANT SOME DINNER?

YER BACK, *HUH?*

KLIK

SNIFF?

WHERE IN THE HECK DID THEY GET THE MONEY TO—

HEY, THIS IS GOOD MEAT.

EVERYONE NEEDS A GOOD MEAL EVERY ONCE IN A WHILE.

NOW, NOW...

LOOK, IF YOU'VE GOT THE MONEY TO SPEND ON STUFF LIKE SUKIYAKI BEEF, HURRY UP AND MOVE OUTTA HERE, WILL YA?

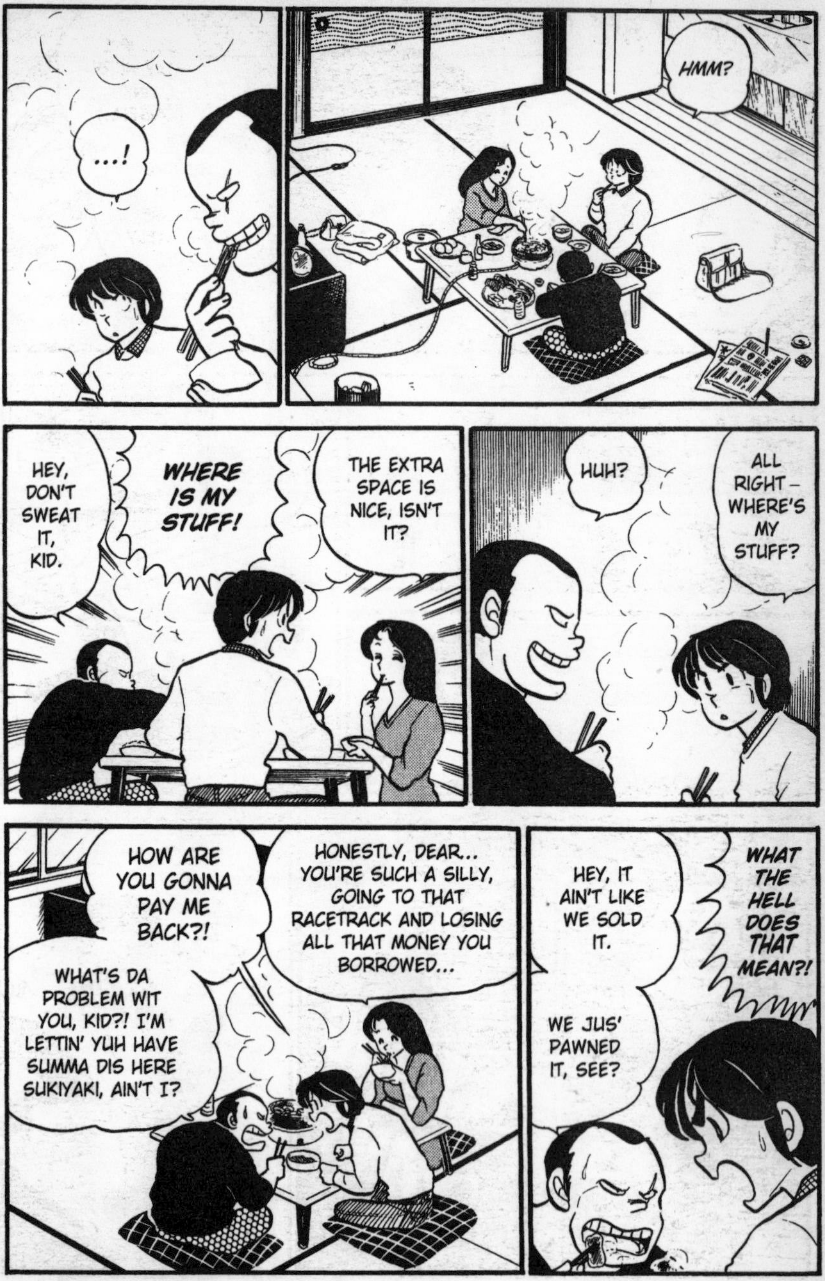
HMM?
...!
ALL RIGHT— WHERE'S MY STUFF?
HUH?
WHERE IS MY STUFF!
THE EXTRA SPACE IS NICE, ISN'T IT?
HEY, DON'T SWEAT IT, KID.
WHAT THE HELL DOES THAT MEAN?!
HEY, IT AIN'T LIKE WE SOLD IT.
WE JUS' PAWNED IT, SEE?
HOW ARE YOU GONNA PAY ME BACK?!
WHAT'S DA PROBLEM WIT YOU, KID?! I'M LETTIN' YUH HAVE SUMMA DIS HERE SUKIYAKI, AIN'T I?
HONESTLY, DEAR... YOU'RE SUCH A SILLY, GOING TO THAT RACETRACK AND LOSING ALL THAT MONEY YOU BORROWED...

IF... IF I STAY HERE ANY LONGER...

THEY'RE GONNA SUCK ME COMPLETELY DRY!

HEY, DAT MEANS DA MORE FER ME, DAT'S WHAT I SAY!

REALLY? DON'T YOU WANT ANY MORE?

I'M GOING OUT AGAIN.

MM? WHAT'S WRONG?

(I ALREADY DID!) OW! HOT!

YUH'LL PAY FER DIS!!

KANG KANG

GOBBLE MUNCH GULP

HEY! HE'S EATIN' ALL DA MEAT!!

205

WHAT A JERK!

YEAH — I DIDN'T THINK HE HAD IT IN HIM.

WOW! YUSAKU...

...IS LIVING WITH A GIRL?!

YEAH, MUST'VE. OTHERWISE, HE'D NEVER HAVE MOVED IN WITH HER SO QUICK!

INDEED. HE MUST HAVE MAINTAINED A RELATIONSHIP WITH THAT WOMAN FOR QUITE SOME TIME.

ER, AKEMI, DEAR — YOU MIND DOING SOME WORK?

HOW COME YOU NEVER TOLD US?!

HUH? YOU MET YUSAKU? WHEN? WHERE?

IT IS MOST ODD... WHEN WE SPOKE RECENTLY, HE SAID NOTHING ABOUT SUCH A RELATIONSHIP.

I AM ASTOUNDED THAT YOU HIRED SUCH AN UNRELIABLE PERSON.

AW, AKEMI ...!

BUT IT TURNS OUT HE'S A JERK JUST LIKE EVERY OTHER GUY. BREAKS MY HEART, SO I GOTTA GET SMASHED.

I SORTA SAW HIM AS A YOUNGER BROTHER...

I MEAN, HE HAD A KINDA CUTE SIDE TO HIM, *HUH?*

WHY SHOULD I?!

WOULD YOU JUST *LISTEN* TO ME?!

...THEN FACE-TO-FACE!

OKAY, IF NOT BY PHONE...

THAP THAP

I'M *NOT* INTERESTED.

LOOK, THAT WOMAN... SHE'S—

WHY, YOU-!

YOU'RE THE ONE RUNNING AROUND LIKE A DOG IN HEAT!!

"FOOL"...? *ME*, A FOOL?!

WOULD YOU SHUT UP AND *LISTEN* TO ME, YOU FOOL?!

AHH!

SMAK

KONK

YOU UNREASON-ABLE BITCH!!

MAYBE I'D BETTER GO THROUGH A THIRD PARTY.

YEAH...

...MAYBE.

I DON'T REALLY THINK IT WOULD GO LIKE THAT, BUT...

OWW...

C'MON IN!

KREEEK

ISH TH' PLAYBOY!

HEY!!

HEY!

208

SAY... YOU'RE ALL PRETTY DRUNK!

YEAH, YOU GOT A LOTTA *GUTSH* COMING 'ROUND HERE!

DON'T TRY T' ACT THE INNOSHENT WITH *ME*, SON!

"PLAY-BOY"...? W-WHAT DO YOU MEAN BY *THAT*?

FWAP

I WILL GLADLY HEAR YOUR TALE.

I AM QUITE SOBER.

HALT, YOUNG MAN.

RUNNIN' AWAY, HUH?! COWARD!

YOU GUYS ARE USELESS.

FORGET IT, THEN.

SO SHE'S A ÷HIC÷ *MARRIED* WOMAN, HUH?

—AND SO SHE WAS JUST LIVING THERE WHEN I ARRIVED. SHE'S GOT A HUSBAND, TOO!

SLRP

IF YOU WILL, IN RETURN, BUY ME A DRINK OR TWO.

YESH, YESH, QUITE SO.

DO *YOU* UNDERSTAND, MR. YOTSUYA?!

I WILL RELAY THESH FACTSH TO OUR MANAGER.

DAMN IT, I TOLD YOU I'M NOT LIVING WITH HER BECAUSE I *WANT* TO!

AN' HE *LIKSH* OLDER WOMEN, TOO!

HUH... SEEMS LIKE YOU GOT A *THING* FOR MARRIED WOMEN.

I MEAN, KYOKO WASH ONCE SOMEBODY'S WIFE, EH?

SLAM

......

......

IT'D BE NICE IF YOU COULD MOVE BACK INTO MAISON IKKOKU...

WELL, I'D BETTER GET MOVING.

"WIFE."

"AYAKO."

"MASSAGE PARLOR."

"I LIKE OLDER WOMEN."

HOWEVER, I THINK I REMEMBER SHERTAIN KEY WORDSH...

......

GLOOOM

NOT AT ALL... I WASH MERELY ENJOYING MY FREE DRINKSH.

SO...÷HIC÷ DIDJA GET WHAT HE WASH TALKIN' ABOUT?

÷HIC÷

CLINK CLINK

HMM.

PERHAPS HE MERELY WISHED TO HAVE THIS INFORMATION PASSED ON TO YOU.

OKAY, SO THIS... THIS *"AYAKO"* PERSON IS MARRIED AND WORKS AT A MASSAGE PARLOR. SO WHAT'S THE POINT HERE?

SO?! SO WHAT?!

I DUNNO... HE DID SAY HE WASN'T LIVING WITH HER OF HIS OWN FREE WILL, OR SOMETHING.

WHAT ARROGANCE — AS IF SHE'S BEGGING HIM TO STAY.

YEAH... MAYBE HE'S JUST KINDA RUBBING YOUR NOSE IN IT 'CAUSE YOU REJECTED HIM?

AT LEAST OUR STORY WAS INTERNALLY CONSISTENT.

WELL... I DON'T THINK SO.

WE DIDN'T LIE, DID WE?

SLAM

THAT... *THAT'S ENOUGH!*

I DON'T WANT TO HEAR ANOTHER WORD!

211

HELLO, KYOKO SPEAKING...

HI, KYOKO? THIS IS YUSAKU.

UMM... I WAS WONDERING IF YOU'D TALKED TO MR. YOTSUYA YET...?

YES, I HAVE.

I NOW UNDERSTAND YOUR CURRENT SITUATION QUITE THOROUGHLY.

SO...UH... WHEN CAN I MOVE BACK?

Y-YOU DO? THAT'S GREAT!

REGRETTABLY, I'VE ALREADY FOUND A NEW TENANT FOR YOUR ROOM.

OH?

UNFORTUNATELY, *ALL* OF THE OPEN ROOMS HAVE BEEN RENTED!

SO... SO HOW ABOUT ROOM 2, OR NUMBER 3?

W**H**A**M**!!

I... I DON'T BELIEVE IT.

MRS. OTONASHI, ISN'T IT?

OH, HELLO!

EXCUSE ME...?

THAT... THAT LITTLE—

I NEVER WANT TO SEE HIS FACE AGAIN!

OH, NO.

IT SOUNDS AS THOUGH THE COUPLE IS TAKING ADVANTAGE OF HIS KINDNESS.

I TELL YOU, HE SEEMS TOTALLY MISERABLE.

I... I SEE.

WHAT?

SO HE'S JUST BOARDING WITH A MARRIED COUPLE?

YOU KNOW... I FIGURED THE STORY WOULDN'T MAKE IT INTACT.

OPEN

COFFEE SNAC

213

NOW I'VE REALLY **DONE** IT.

WHAT A DISASTER.

SSHH

......

SSHH

HEH... WE KIND OF FOUND OUT THE **REAL** STORY FROM THE GUY AT CHA CHA MARU.

Y-YES...? WHAT IS IT?

EXCUSE US...

GOOD NEWS, *EH*, KYOKO?! LET'S CELEBRATE WITH A LI'L DRINKIE!

YOU KNOW, I'M REALLY HAPPY. YUSAKU *IS* AS NAÏVE AS I ALWAYS THOUGHT.

BLUP BLUP

WELL, YEAH, BUT WE WERE COMPLETELY DRUNK.

WHAT DO YOU MEAN, THE "REAL STORY"...? I THOUGHT YOU WERE ALL THERE LISTENING TO YUSAKU.

"UNFORTUNATELY, ALL OF THE OPEN ROOMS HAVE BEEN RENTED!"

I DON'T BELIEVE IT.

IT'S GOTTA BE A JOKE.

THIS REALLY IS A DISASTER!

EH?!

SSHH!

BOWF?

AW, C'MON, KYOKO!! QUIT CLEANING UP!

THAT'S SO *BORING* !!

NO, WAIT-!

SOUNDS LIKE THEY'RE HAVING A WELCOMING PARTY...

BWAHAW

HEE HA-HEE HA-HA

THERE'S A... A LIGHT IN MY ROOM!

THEN... THEN IT *WAS* TRUE.

HA HA HA HA

THIS WAS ALL MY FAULT...

YUSAKU, PLEASE COME BACK.

NOW I'M REALLY ALL ALONE...

HEE HEE

AKEMI !!

BLOOSH

PART ELEVEN
DOWN THE HOME STRETCH

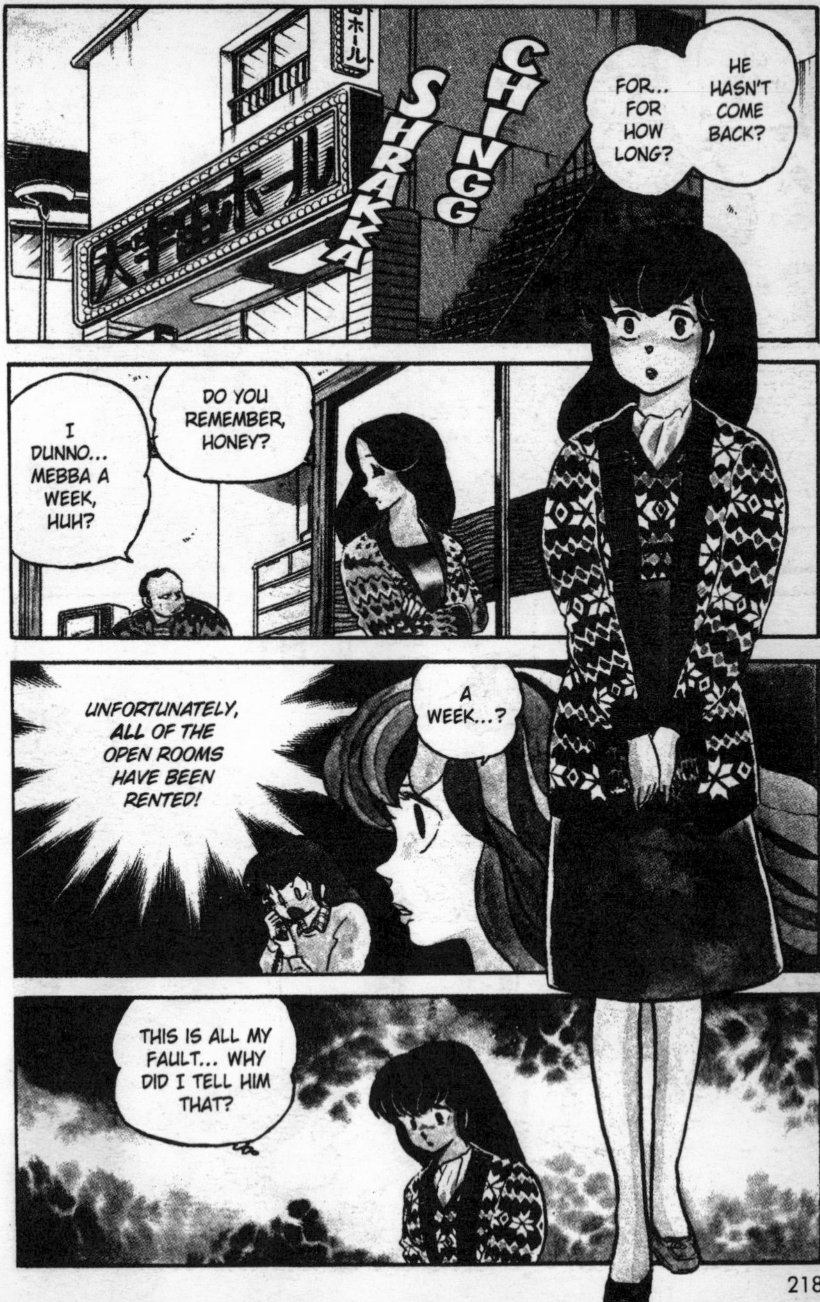
SHRAKKA
CHINGG
HE HASN'T COME BACK?
FOR... FOR HOW LONG?
DO YOU REMEMBER, HONEY?
I DUNNO... MEBBA A WEEK, HUH?
A WEEK...?
UNFORTUNATELY, ALL OF THE OPEN ROOMS HAVE BEEN RENTED!
THIS IS ALL MY FAULT... WHY DID I TELL HIM THAT?

OH, YUSAKU...

SO... UH... WHEN CAN I MOVE BACK?

KYOKO...?

WHERE COULD HE HAVE GONE?

NOW WHAT DO I DO?

I'M SO SORRY...

IT'S GOTTEN QUITE CHILLY, LATELY.

YES.

HWOOOOO

UM... NO.

KLAKK

SO, HAVE YOU HEARD FROM YUSAKU?

219

I... I DON'T KNOW.

WHAT DO YOU THINK?

I WONDER WHY HE HASN'T CONTACTED US...?

......

......

OF COURSE.

CAN I HAVE SOME MORE?

SLRPP

......

KLAKK

SPLSSH

I REALLY WONDER WHY YUSAKU HASN'T COME BACK...

SSHH

W-WHAT? WHAT?

HEY, YOU!

......

LOOK, MAYBE YOU CAN FOOL THE REST OF THE WORLD, BUT I KNOW YOU BETTER THAN THAT.

ALL RIGHT, WHAT DID YOU DO?

W-WHAT DO YOU MEAN?

B... BUT...

SO WHAT HAPPENED?

C'MON, YOU CAN TELL ME.

WELL, THEN...

YOU REALLY THINK SO?

LOOK, IF I KNOW SOMETHING HAPPENED, MAYBE WE CAN DO SOMETHING ABOUT IT...

...IF WE PUT OUR HEADS TOGETHER.

B-BUT I...

W-WHAT?! YOU TOLD HIM ALL THE ROOMS WERE RENTED?!?

HEY, AKEMI, LISTEN TO *THIS!!*

MORNING.

B-BUT...

SO *THAT'S* WHY HE HASN'T COME BACK.

WHAAAT? JEEZ, KYOKO, WHAT AN AWFUL THING TO SAY!

WELL, YEAH, OKAY... TRUE.

BECAUSE... WELL, YOU *ALL* TOLD ME HE WAS BRAGGING ABOUT LIVING WITH THIS "AYAKO" PERSON.

SHIK

OH, YEAH?

IT'S PARTLY *YOUR* FAULT, TOO, AKEMI!!

YEAH... WHY SHOULD A MANAGER CARE ABOUT A TENANT'S PERSONAL LIFE, ANYWAY?

BUT...

HONESTLY, KYOKO... WHY'D YOU HAVE TO TELL HIM SUCH AN AWFUL LIE?

LET'S PUT OUR HEAD'S TOGETHER AND—

OKAY, NOW THAT YOU KNOW WHAT HAPPENED...

LOOK, THIS ISN'T THE TIME FOR SUCH NONSENSE!

SURE DOES.

Y'KNOW... THIS LOOKS LIKE A LOVER'S SPAT, DOESN'T IT?

BUT DON'T YOU FEEL BETTER HAVING GOTTEN IT OFF YOUR CHEST?

HERE I TOLD YOU EVERYTHING, AND NOW YOU JUST—

BUT...

FORGET IT — THIS LOOKS PRETTY HOPELESS TO ME.

WHY DID I EVEN OPEN MY MOUTH?!

SLAM

YEAH, MAYBE WE JUST BETTER FORGET ABOUT HIM.

223

WATCH WHERE YOU'RE GOING, IDIOT!

B'MP

WHAT IF HE GETS DESPERATE AND...

ASK ME IF I CARE, YOU GODDAMN JERK!

SNIK

HEY, PAL... YOU DISRE-SPECTIN' ME?

HYAAARGGH!

THEN DIE, PUNK!

HWOOOOO

N-NO... NOT THAT!

K... KYOKO...

TWIST TWIST

=SNIFF=
=SNORK=

HAA-CHOO!!

MAN, YOU ARE SICK AS A DOG.

=SNIFF=

BLOSH

OF COURSE I GOT A COLD...

...IT WAS FREEZING COLD THAT NIGHT.

HA-CHOO!

KANG KANG

HYOOOO

SNZZ SNORE

NOK NOK

HELLO-OOO... HEY, LET ME IN!

NOK NOK!

I FORGOT TO TAKE MY KEYS.

UH-OH.

KCHAK

MAN. I'M GONNA FREEZE TO DEATH!

SHIVER SHAKE

S-SORRY, MA'AM.

QUIET OR I'M CALLIN' THE COPS!

I DUNNO... BUT I AIN'T GOING BACK TO LIVE WITH THOSE TWO BLOODSUCKERS.

SO NOW WHAT ARE YOU GONNA DO?

H-HI... S-SAKAMOTO? I-I-I'M D-DYING...

WHOA, BUDDY, HANG IN THERE – WHAT'S UP?

CRYING YOURSELF TO SLEEP?

-SNIFF-

GUESS I'LL LOOK FOR A NEW PLACE...

YOU SURE YOU CAN'T JUST GO BACK TO MAISON IKKOKU?

NO...

...THERE ARE NO ROOMS LEFT.

IT WAS ALL MY OWN DAMN FAULT TO BEGIN WITH.

ANYWAY, I'M SURE TO FIND A PLACE IN A COUPLE OF DAYS.

-SNURK-

YEAH, AND THE MANAGER'S KINDA A COLD FISH, TOO, HUH?

AW, SHUDDAP

I DUNNO, SAKAMOTO... I'VE ALREADY BEEN HERE A WEEK.

WELL, DON'T WORRY— YOU CAN CAMP OUT HERE UNTIL THEN.

YOU'RE A PAL.

WELL, OKAY.

-SZNXX-

YEAH, BUT I REALLY SHOULDN'T...

FORGET IT, I SAID.

 YUSAKU GODAI?

KYOKO HERE. *UMM... IS* YUSAKU THERE?

TODAY'S THE DAY HE TUTORS IKUKO, RIGHT?

 HELLO, MR. OTONASHI ...?

 HIS VOICE SOUNDED TERRIBLE.

 WELL, DEAR, HE CALLED IN TO CANCEL – SAID HE HAD A BAD COLD.

N-NO... FORGET IT. THANKS, MR. OTONASHI.

 DID SOMETHING HAPPEN TO HIM?

HE SOUNDED LIKE HE WAS AT DEATH'S DOOR, IN MY OPINION.

ISN'T HE THERE?

 HE... HE'S REALLY SICK?

 KOFF KOFF

HWOOOO

I WONDER WHY...?

 SICK...

KLIK

KANGG

K... KYOKO...

KOFF KOFF KOFF

KOFF STAGGER

WOOD

HWOOOO

N-NO... NOT THAT!

...SO I COULD APOLOGIZE.

IF I COULD ONLY SEE HIM JUST ONCE MORE...

HOW COME THINGS HAD TO TURN OUT LIKE THIS?

WURF BOWF

MR. SOICHIRO, WHAT SHOULD I DO...?

HOW *COULD* I HAVE SAID SUCH THINGS TO HIM?

BUT HE'LL PROBABLY NEVER CALL AGAIN.

SNZZ GZNZZ

I CAN'T REALLY EXPECT MOM AND DAD TO HELP ME OUT OF THIS ONE, EITHER.

FIRST, I GOTTA FIND A NEW PART-TIME JOB.

I CAN HARDLY AFFORD ANYTHING...

HWOOO

~SNIFF~

~SNRRK~

FWMP WHUD KSSH

?

NOK NOK

~SNRFF~

YO, SAKA-MOTO!

LEMME IN.

230

TUMP
TUMP
TUMP

NOK
NOK

SAKAMOTO

HWOOOO

HAA-CHOO!

OH. "GIRL-FRIEND," HUH?

::SNFF::

TOIK

WHAT'S UP?

GEE, YOU'RE EARLY.

CHAK

UH, HI.

JUST TAKE YOUR TIME, OKAY?

THANKS FOR LETTING ME STAY.

I'VE GOT ANOTHER PLACE TO GO.

SORRY, YUSAKU, BUT YOU MIND CATCHING A MOVIE OR SOMETHING?

HEY, HEY, NO PROBLEM.

HAA-CHOO!!

HWOOOOO

231

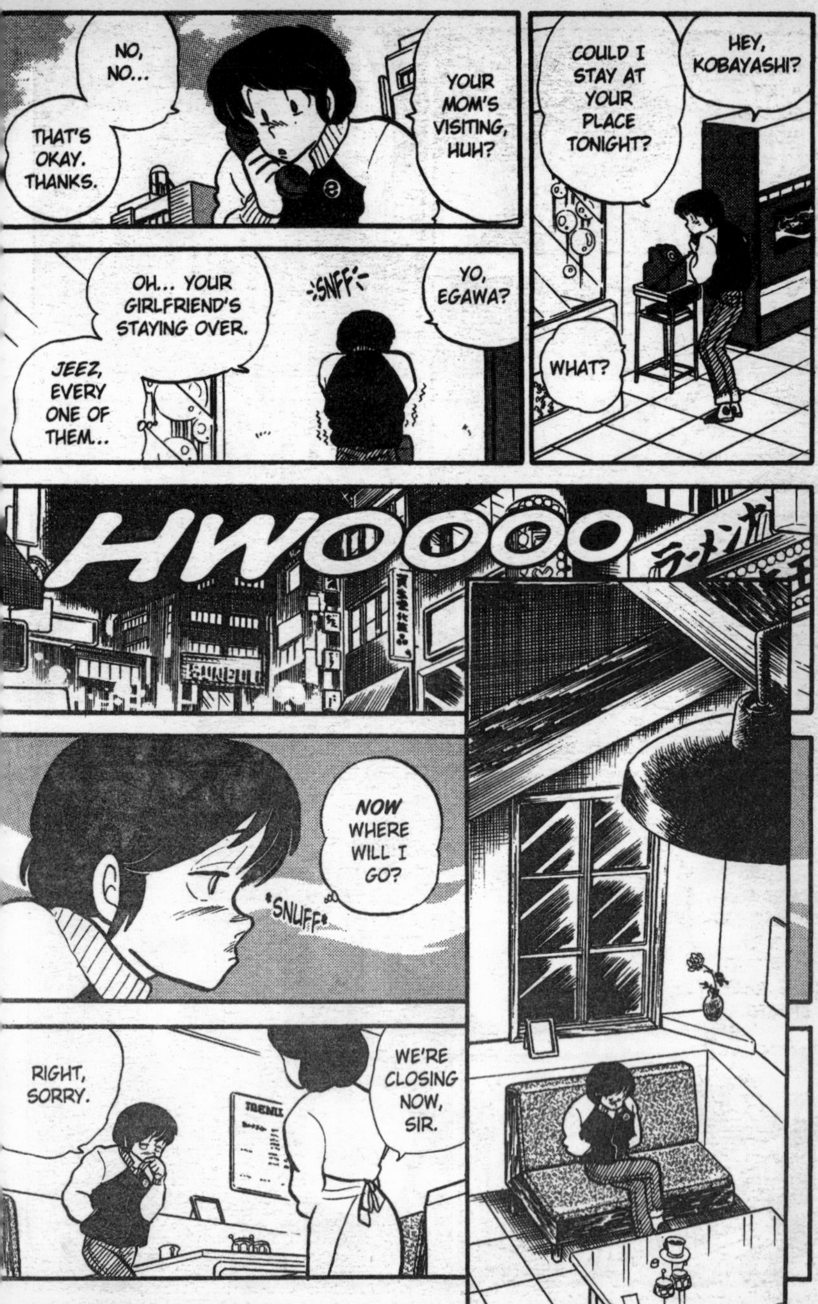
HEY, KOBAYASHI?
COULD I STAY AT YOUR PLACE TONIGHT?
WHAT?
YOUR MOM'S VISITING, HUH?
NO, NO...
THAT'S OKAY. THANKS.
YO, EGAWA?
SNFF
OH... YOUR GIRLFRIEND'S STAYING OVER.
JEEZ, EVERY ONE OF THEM...
HWOOOO
NOW WHERE WILL I GO?
SNUFF
WE'RE CLOSING NOW, SIR.
RIGHT, SORRY.

DAMN... NOT ENOUGH MONEY!

UH-OH!

GUESS I MAY AS WELL JUST GO TO AN ALL-NIGHT MOVIE...

OH, WELL...

HWOOO

BRRRRR

HWOOOOOO

HWOOOO

YOU REALLY DON'T HAVE A PLACE FOR ME ANYMORE, KYOKO...?

KYOKO...

INDEED. THE ENTIRE PURPOSE OF OUR INVITATION WAS TO ATTEMPT TO RAISE YOUR SPIRITS.

YOU'LL FEEL BETTER IF YOU HAVE ONE.

COME ON, KYOKO – HAVE A DRINK.

PERSONALLY, I FIGURE THE WHOLE BUNCH OF YOU ARE GUILTY.

OH, YEAH?

IT WASN'T REALLY *ANYBODY'S* FAULT.

LOOK, MOPING WON'T HELP ANYTHING.

BOWF?

HWOOOO

IF I DRINK, I'LL JUST START CRYING...

I SHOULDN'T.

THAT'S A GOOD BOY!

SEEMS LIKE YOU REMEMBER ME, HUH?

HEY, MR. SOICHIRO.

BOWF BOWF

FFT FFT

LOOKS LIKE EVERYONE'S OUT...

-:HIC:-

DESPITE YOUR PROTEST-ATIONS, YOU CERTAINLY CONSUMED A GREAT DEAL OF ALCOHOL.

ARE YOU OKAY, KYOKO?

...EVEN THOUGH IT ISN'T REALLY HOME ANYMORE.

MY FEET JUST TOOK ME HERE...

BOWF!

WHSSK

EEP!

HEY, YOU! WHAT ARE YOU UP TO?

A BURGLAR, ISN'T IT?!

THAT'S...

HOLD IT RIGHT THERE! HELP, THIEF!

YU...

PLEASE STOP!

KYOKO, DON'T!!

YUSAKU!

GO AWAY!

WAIT!!

D-DID SHE SAY "YUSAKU" ...?

I DON'T WANT TO LIVE WITH YOU ANYMORE!!

I SAID LEAVE ME ALONE!!

I WILL NOT!!

YOU STOP *RIGHT* NOW!

BUT THAT'S WHAT I—

VWHIP

YUSAKU GODAI!!

YEAH... WHY *AM I* RUNNING AWAY, ANYHOW?

SNF *SNRK*

DON'T YOU *DARE* RUN AWAY FROM ME!!

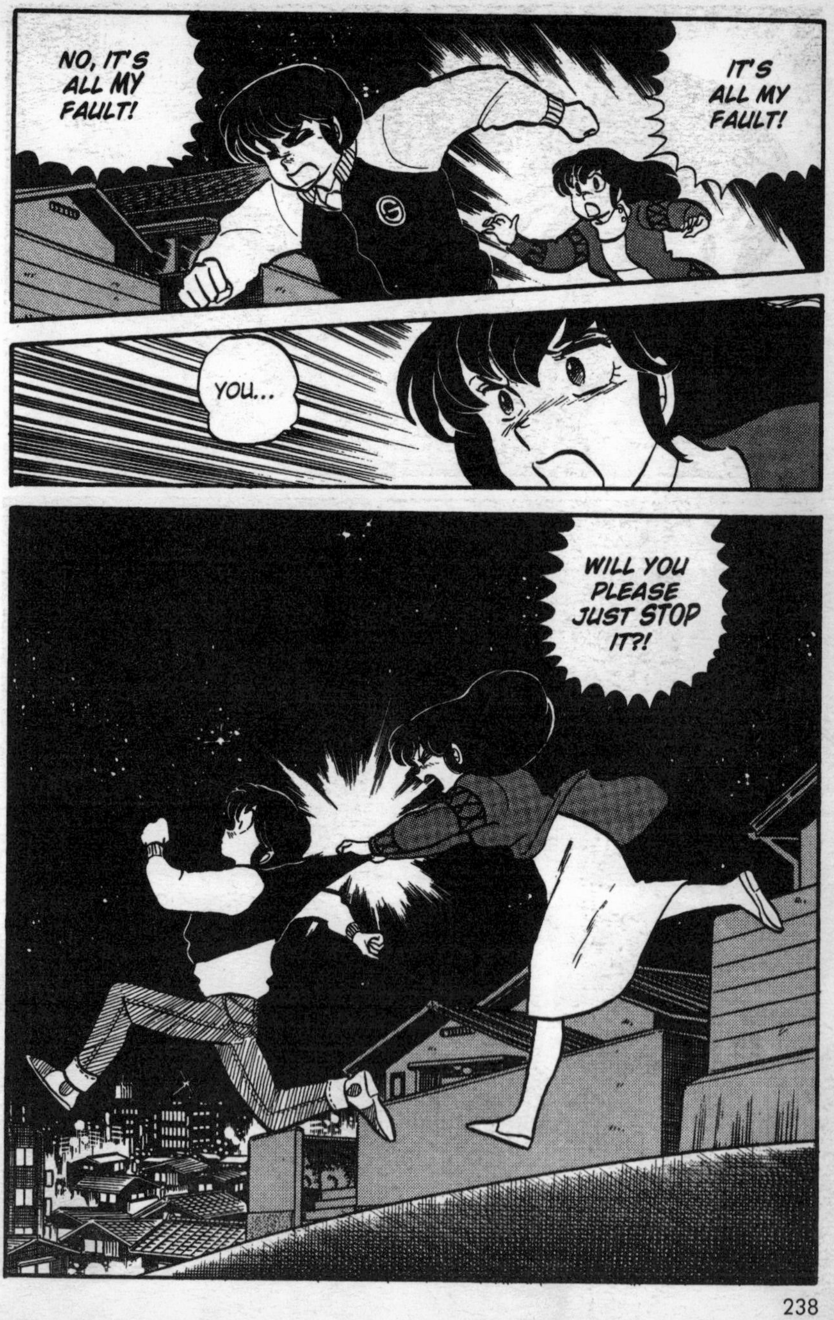
NO, IT'S ALL MY FAULT!
IT'S ALL MY FAULT!
YOU...
WILL YOU PLEASE JUST STOP IT?!

HUFF HUFF

HAHH HAHH

-SNURFF-

-SNFF-

OH, YUSAKU, **PLEASE** COME BACK!

K... KYOKO...

WAAHH!

.....

I'VE GOT... I'VE GOT ROOMS ...

EEP!

·····

D-DON'T C-CRY! ÷SNFF÷ PLEASE DON'T CRY!

AAHUH-HUH!

YAAAHH!

EEP!

÷SNIFF÷ ÷SNIFF÷

HWOOOOO

IF I'D HAD A CHOICE, I THINK I'D HAVE PREFERRED TO COME BACK HOME WITH A BIT MORE DIGNITY...

WELL, AT LEAST YOU HAVE RETURNED.

GOD, WHAT A SLOB... HERE'S A TISSUE.

÷SNIFF÷ ÷SNIFF÷

SLSSH

CAN WE GET A MOVE ON HERE, PLEASE?

DO YOU MIND WALKING A BIT FASTER?

WHAT ARE YOU TWO DOING?!

C'MON, LET'S GO HOME.

fushigi yûgi ™

VOLUMES 1-10 OUT NOW!

Welcome to the wonderfully exciting, funny, and heartfelt tale of
Miaka Yûki, a normal high-school girl who is suddenly whisked
away into a fictional version of ancient China.

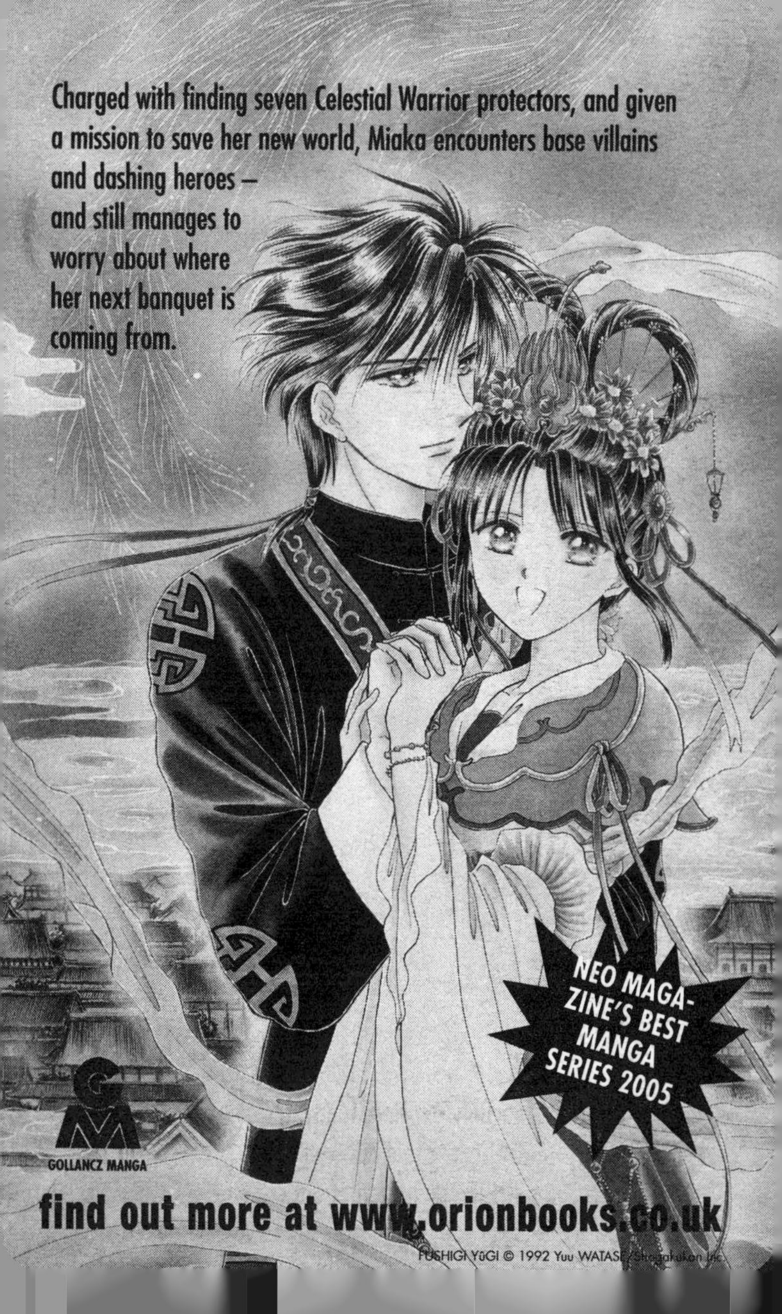
Charged with finding seven Celestial Warrior protectors, and given a mission to save her new world, Miaka encounters base villains and dashing heroes – and still manages to worry about where her next banquet is coming from.
NEO MAGAZINE'S BEST MANGA SERIES 2005
GOLLANCZ MANGA
find out more at www.orionbooks.co.uk
FUSHIGI YûGI © 1992 Yuu WATASE/Shogakukan Inc.

MEET JIMMY KUDO.

Ace high-school student with keen powers of observation, he helps police solve the baffling crimes . . . until, hot on the trial of a suspect, he's accosted and fed a strange chemical which transforms him into a puny grade schooler!

Spooky crimes, baffling robberies, and comic would-be detectives, no crime's too tough to crack for Jimmy! ... especially not his personal case: to find the mysterious masked men and make them change him back ... All the clues are here — can you solve the case before Jimmy does?

VOLUMES 1-9 OUT NOW!

GOLLANCZ MANGA

find out more at www.orionbooks.co.uk

FLAME OF RECCA

Demons, battles, mysteries and excitement abound in the adventures of Recca, Domon, Fuko and Yanagi.

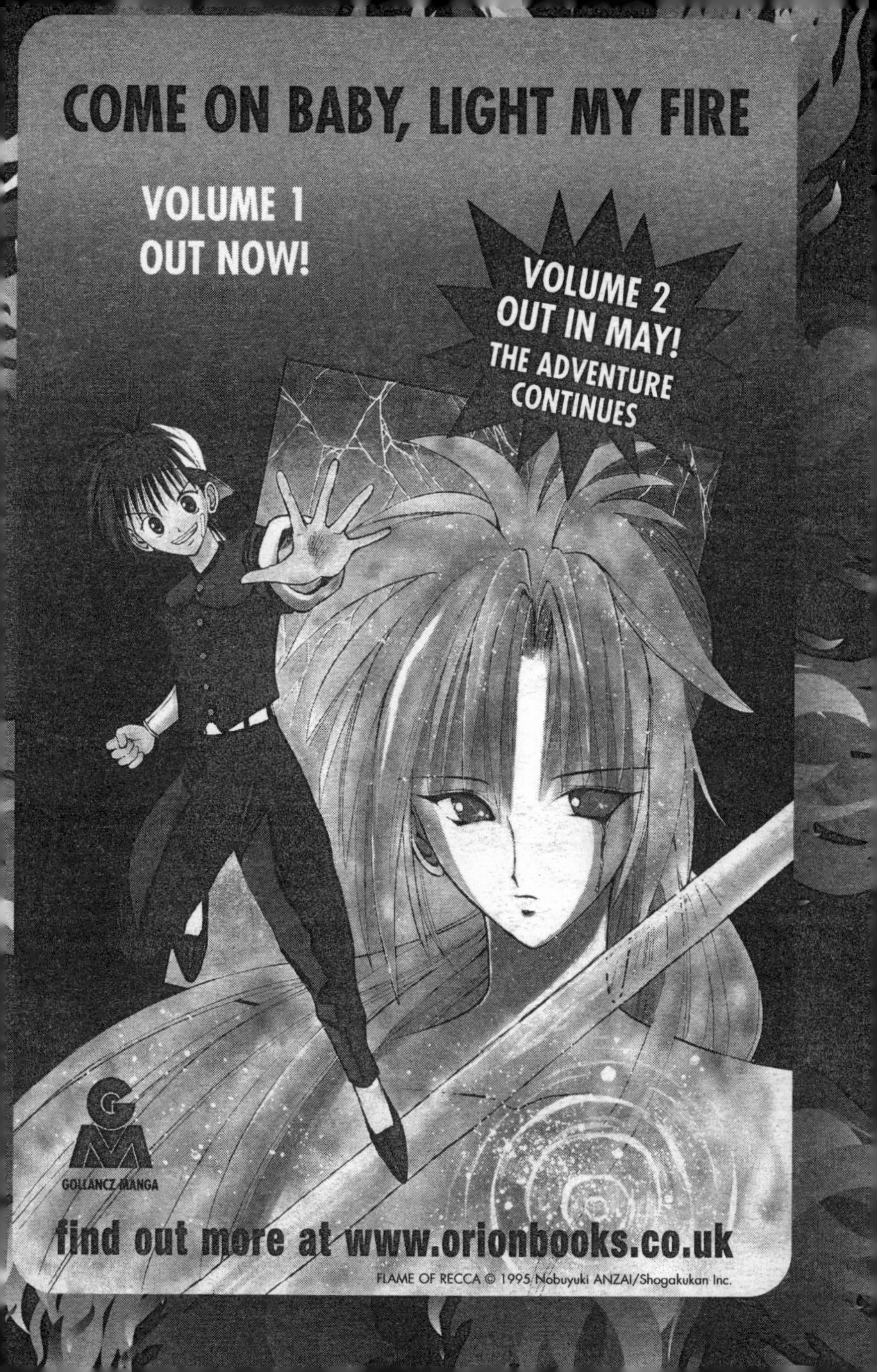
COME ON BABY, LIGHT MY FIRE
VOLUME 1
OUT NOW!
VOLUME 2
OUT IN MAY!
THE ADVENTURE
CONTINUES
GOLLANCZ MANGA
find out more at www.orionbooks.co.uk
FLAME OF RECCA © 1995 Nobuyuki ANZAI/Shogakukan Inc.

maison ikkoku ™

THE UNMISSABLE NEW GOLLANCZ MANGA SERIES STARTS HERE!

Yusaku's attempts to study get off to a bad start when he falls head-over-heels for the new manager, and he's a long, long way from winning her heart. For Kyoko already has somebody else on her mind . . . a mysterious "Mr. Soichiro" . . .

VOLUMES 1-4 OUT NOW!

From Rumiko Takahashi, the princess of manga and the creator of *Inuyasha* and *Ranma 1/2*, *Maison Ikkoku* is a love story that takes place in Japan, but could take place anywhere.

fushigi yûgi ™

OUT IN MAY!

Vol. **11**: VETERAN

Veteran

Miaka and her friend-turned-mortal-enemy Yui are locked in a race to find the last Shentso-Pao, but locating the treasure is more difficult than they anticipated: Xi-Lang isn't a frozen wasteland of forgotten dreams and ghosts, like Bei-Jai. It's a vibrant, living desert country, whose inhabitants are veterans of the last clash between priestesses and gods!

GOLLANCZ MANGA

find out more at www.orionbooks.co.uk

CASE CLOSED™

CASE CLOSED
Story and art by
Gosho Aoyama
Vol. 9

OUT IN APRIL!

Conan Edogawa, ace detective, is springing into action again! The Junior Detective league embark on a lethal game of hide-and-seek, there's a murderous birthday party, and a mysterious 'suicide' . . . Can you solve his cases before Conan does?

GOLLANCZ MANGA

find out more at www.orionbooks.co.uk

ABOUT THE ARTIST

Rumiko Takahashi, born in 1957 in Niigata, Japan, is the acclaimed creator and artist of *Maison Ikkoku, InuYasha, Ranma 1/2* and *Lum * Urusei Yatsura*.

She lived in a small student's apartment in Nakano, Japan, which was the basis for the *Maison Ikkoku* series, while she attended the prestigious Nihon Joseidai (Japan Women's University). At the same time, Takahashi also began studying comics at Gekiga Sonjuku, a famous school for manga artists run by Kazuo Koike, author of *Crying Freeman* and *Lone Wolf and Cub*. In 1978, Takahashi won a prize in Shogakukan's annual New Comic Artist Contest and her boy-meets-alien comedy *Lum * Urusei Yatsura* began appearing in the weekly manga magazine *Shonen Sunday*.

Takahashi's success and critical acclaim continues to grow, with popular titles including *Ranma 1/2* and *InuYasha*. Many of her graphic novel series have also been animated, and are widely available in several languages.

MAISON IKKOKU

VOLUME 4
Gollancz Manga Edition
Story and art by Rumiko Takahashi

Translation/Gerard Jones & Matt Thorn
Touch-up & Lettering/Susan Daigle-Leach
Design/Nozomi Akashi
Editors-1st Edition/Satoru Fujii & Trish Ledoux
Editors-2nd Edition/Elizabeth Kawasaki
UK Cover Adaptation/Sue Michniewicz

10 9 8 7 6 5 4 3 2 1

The right of Rumiko Takahashi to be identified as the author of this
work has been asserted by her in accordance with the Copyright,
Designs and Patents Act 1988.

A CIP catalogue record for this book is
available from the British Library.

ISBN 0 57507 839 1
ISBN 9 780 57507 839 0

Printed and bound at Mackays of Chatham, plc,
Chatham, Kent

PARENTAL ADVISORY
Maison Ikkoku is rated T+ for Teen Plus. Contains realistic and
graphic violence. Recommended for older teens (16 and up).

The Orion Publishing Group's policy is to use papers that
are natural, renewable and recyclable products and made
from wood grown in sustainable forests. The logging and
manufacturing processes are expected to conform to the
environmental regulations of the country of origin.

www.orionbooks.co.uk